Mayo Finirly Rathfan,
June 1947.

The Marble Man's Wife

by Hayden Norwood

This is a "conversational biography" of Mrs. Julia Wolfe, mother of Thomas Wolfe. Mrs. Wolfe died in the spring of 1946 just a few weeks before her 86th birthday. Mr. Norwood, an Allentown, Pennsylvania, newspaper man, gathered the material from Mrs. Wolfe not long before she died. He spent some time in Asheville, N. C., at the Wolfe homestead, and Mrs. Wolfe was his guest at his home in Pennsylvania.

As the original of "Eliza Gant" in Thomas Wolfe's "Look Homeward, Angel," "Of Time and the River," and other novels, Mrs. Wolfe is known to hundreds of thousands of readers. But the actual story of her life, minus fictional embroidery, is quite as interesting, amusing, and earthy as Thomas Wolfe's treatment of her in his novels. Mrs. Wolfe was a little, compact, wiry woman, with an inflexible determination, a prodigious memory, and a stupendous gift of speech.

Mrs. Wolfe could "talk the hinges off a barn door," and everything she said was fascinating. Mr. Norwood's book is made up almost entirely of these conversations. They deal with Mrs. Wolfe's childhood, with Mr. Wolfe, with Thomas Wolfe's brothers and sisters, with domestic crises, with business deals, and with a hundred and one homey, pungent matters that concern an American family made famous through Wolfe's pictures of them in his books.

With Mr. Norwood interposing a question now and then, and with Mrs. Wolfe going full spate the reader gets a complete, and completely fascinating, picture of a personality. All of the Thomas Wolfe audience will enjoy this book to the last word. It includes many stories about Wolfe never before told and an immense amount of information about the American backgrounds of his novels and their characters.

THE
MARBLE MAN'S
WIFE

THE MARBLE MAN'S WIFE

Thomas Wolfe's Mother

By

Hayden Norwood

CHARLES SCRIBNER'S SONS
New York · 1947

To

MY GOOD FRIEND

Fred W. Weiler

of the

ALLENTOWN MORNING CALL

Foreword

The other day I read of the passing of Mrs. Julia Wolfe, immortal Thomas Wolfe's mother. She was just a few weeks shy of her eighty-sixth birthday. Reading her obituary I felt not exactly shock, but a curious let-down, as if a trusted friend had got caught cheating. For one did not think of Mrs. Wolfe as one to die, certainly not under a hundred years. She used to speak with such complacency, quiet contempt almost, of the flagging, sickening and death of others who were old.

And now she herself had tripped. But it might have been worse, a cancer, a slipping memory, something base and stupid. The way it was, she died with her boots on, in the heart of New York City's swarming hive, talking and talking till the wee small hours.

Chapter One

The April sun shone warmly that afternoon I went with the mother of Thomas Wolfe to the cemetery. The polished Vermont granite of Thomas Wolfe's marker was warm as firm living flesh when I placed my hand upon it. But there was more than a hint of chill to the air when clouds dark on their bellies cut off the sunshine now and again.

His mother—a small, compact, well-preserved woman in her eighty-third year—had brought with her lilies of the valley and gladioli bulbs to place in the earth above the graves. She had brought, too, a large paper sack of rich earth from her own yard, to scatter upon a number of arid, bare patches.

She said, without boast, but with the quiet satisfaction of assurance, "Everything I put in the ground will grow. It's always been that way, since I was a girl —way back there when I was about six years old, when Father bought a hundred acres on the Swannanoa. We had a mountain field there. Not many weeds, but the ground was rich. I said to my brother Jim, 'Come

1

on, Jim, give me all your seeds and I'll put them in.
I'll put in the beans and the pumpkins and squash.'

"And I put a seed in every hill and covered it up,
and we rushed along and got them all planted. We
didn't go back up there until later, in the fall. My
brother Henry was up there with his gun, hunting, and
he came back all upset, and said, 'You can't walk or
take a step. There are pumpkins and vines everywhere. She didn't have a bit of sense. She has put a
seed in every hill of corn. The beans are hanging in
clusters, and you can't walk for the pumpkins.'

"And I said to Jim, 'Jim!—let's go up there to see.'
And we did. I can still see that pumpkin field. They
were just everywhere—the vines. Mother said, 'You
will have to gather them now for the winter. We can
use the dried beans in the winter.'

"But that was a job I didn't like, to pull those dried
beans. We would take a big table cloth and jump on
them with our feet and shatter them out that way."

Thomas Wolfe's mother felt of her nose thoughtfully with fingers earth-browned. She laughed, a quiet
"Hah!" Her small eyes shone mischievously.

"I was always telling big hobgoblin stories," she
said. "There was one little knoll at that place where
a little water drained down. But in severe dry weather
there was only a black greasy streak, and that little
ridge was red, and nothing would grow a foot high
there. And Jim said, 'It looks like grease.' And I said,
'The Indians used to live all around here. That mound

is where they buried all those Indians, and that is the grease that is running out of the bones. That is what makes that black greasy streak.' You couldn't get my brother Will to go back there after that. They believed anything I told them."

She bent, covered a bulb with earth. In a minute she straightened again, and regarded me fixedly.

"I have always wanted to go back there. I have often wondered if there was mineral in that hill. Oil maybe. I remember that greasy streak. There wasn't anything living up there to make a greasy streak . . . But oh, those raspberries that grew around those rocks —the old blue raspberries!"

She drew a step closer and thrust out her index finger in the masculine gesture familiar to all who have met Eliza Gant in Thomas Wolfe's first two novels. She said,

"Why, I tell you, those were the primitive days. One Sunday afternoon we were up there on the plateau gathering berries, and I know there wasn't anything obstructing the view, and all of a sudden there were three old wolves smelling along, and I said, 'Let's run —let's go back to the house—and don't let Brute'— that was the dog—'see the wolves!' I was afraid, you know, that he'd bark and then the wolves would see us.

"We went down that mountain in a hurry. Father and Henry went up with their guns, but the wolves had gone. That night we could hear them howling though. Did you ever hear a wolf? Wh-o-o-o! Like that. Say, did you ever hear a wildcat?"

She shook her head, a short, convulsive movement, her lips pursed.

"Those were the primitive days. There wasn't any such word in the language as frigidaire. No radios. No telephones. We heard news weeks after it happened. You don't know how it was then."

She was silent now, stooping, her fingers probing familiarly in the earth. The sun no longer shone now. The day had turned gray with April suddenness. I looked at the tombstones with the unceasing awe all must feel who have read about W. O. Gant, the spree-drinking monument cutter, and Ben Gant of the fierce scowl and tender heart, and Eugene, who was Thomas himself. And here they lie buried. On the big stone:

W. O. WOLFE
Born at Gettysburg, Pa.
April 10, 1851
Died June 20, 1922

Next to the big stone is the one the tourists come to see:

TOM
SON OF
W. O. AND JULIA E.
WOLFE
A BELOVED AMERICAN AUTHOR
OCT. 3, 1900—SEPT. 15, 1938

"The last voyage, the longest, the best."
Look Homeward, Angel
"Death bent to touch his chosen son with
Mercy, love and pity, and put the seal
Of honor on him when he died."
The Web and the Rock

Not far distant are two modest stones:

GROVER C. WOLFE
Oct. 27, 1892
Nov. 16, 1904

And:

BEN H. WOLFE
Oct. 27, 1892
Oct. 19, 1918

These were the twins—Grover, who died tragically in St. Louis, and Ben, whom Thomas Wolfe loved probably more than anyone else on earth.

His mother straightened from her work.

"Say, speaking of the old days—the first electric lights." She laughed, a quiet snickering, passing a finger beneath her nose. "I went north with Mr. Wolfe after we were married. We went to Richmond, Baltimore, Washington City, Philadelphia. Nothing but gas, gas, gas lights. No electric lights. Well, we got to this

5

old rambling hotel in Harrisburg, Pennsylvania. The United States Hotel. They had had electric lights put in. The first time I had ever seen them in a bedroom before. They had a light coming down from the ceiling just about the foot of our bed. Mr. Wolfe went to bed first, and was lying there and I was ready for bed, and he said, 'What are you going to do about that light?' I said, 'You know you have to turn it out. You can't blow it out.' Mr. Wolfe said he knew that. 'Why didn't you ask them about it downstairs?' I asked him.

"Well, we talked about it and finally I climbed down to the foot of the bed. I said to Mr. Wolfe, 'Give me your handkerchief.' And he said, 'What do you want with the handkerchief?' I said, 'I've heard cotton is a non-conductor. I'm going to fold it up and touch this light and see what happens.'

"I took the handkerchief and went quietly and easy about that light, and I touched that button and found nothing happened. I turned it and the light went out. Mr. Wolfe said, 'What are you going to do now if we have to have a light in the night?' I turned it back on. And I stayed there for a little bit, turning it back and forth, never saying a word. Finally I turned it off and crawled back and I said, 'That didn't hurt.' It tickled Mr. Wolfe, and when we got home he told about it, and I started telling the story on him. He was just afraid, that was it."

She bent to her work now with a will. I felt a drop of rain upon the back of my neck, another presently.

Thomas Wolfe's mother said, "Times have changed." She regarded me intently, fixedly. "Most of my friends are out in the cemetery. They have passed on. Look—take Woodfin Street and Spruce Street. The people who lived on those streets used to be good representative citizens. From the hospital down to the Y. M. C. A. building they were all good citizens fifty to sixty years ago. I knew them all. We all visited. But there isn't one person living of them all today—except Julia E. Wolfe. That's how a town changes in less than fifty years. You can take every street, I suppose, and find it the same way. The people have died, and new people have taken their places. From the Square to the Post-office—well, take College Street clear up to Beau-catcher tunnel—there is only one person on that street who lived there forty years ago. That is Mrs. Pegram. The rest have all gone—moved away, or died. I'm speaking about the time when Mr. Wolfe and I were married. Some of them were older than I at that time. A great many were younger, but they are all gone."

"It's raining, Mrs. Wolfe," I said.

She peered up at the torn, dark clouds. In a moment she was busy placing lilies of the valley in the earth. The drops were falling faster; I said to myself that she might, if she hurried, finish before getting very wet.

I went to the automobile and got my topcoat out of the back seat.

"Here, Mrs. Wolfe, you'd better put this on."

She straightened up. She looked at me sharply, then

at the coat, and then at me again. She shook her head firmly.

"I'll put it around your shoulders," I said.

"No, I don't want it."

I held the coat over my arm, watching her as she moved slowly, with contemplative expression, among the graves. She paused near the high boxwood shrubs.

"These boxwoods," she said, "are over fifty years old. Way back there—I had some friends out in the country who had rooted out some of that boxwood, and they sent me a couple of dozen. I set the little bushes out . . . It was on my first property . . . You know, I bought this lot over on Chestnut Street. Oh, they thought I was the smartest girl in town! Old Judge Aston was in the fire insurance business, and he was selling off those lots, one hundred and two hundred feet deep, and Father bought the second lot from the corner. He wrote me and said, 'I've bought the lot and I'm building us a home.' I was ambitious. I had saved up $125—had it over there in the mountains where I was teaching school. I wrote Father a letter, saying, 'Here's $125—if they won't trust me for the other $25, you pay it for me. I want you to buy me that corner lot next to yours.'

"Well, Father went down and read the letter to Judge Aston, and the old judge says, 'But the corner lot is $200. It's one of the more expensive lots.' Father said, 'Well, she didn't know. I told her I paid $150 for mine and she wanted the one next to it. I'll just send her money back to her.'

"Old Judge scratched his head, and says, 'There isn't a man in this town would get that lot for less than $200, but doggone it, Miss Julia is going to get it for $150. Any girl that will work and save up her money like that has got to be favored.'

"So Father paid the other $25 and I paid him. After the first year I had to pay the taxes on it. They sent a notice out. I got the tax notice on that lot—forty-eight cents. I read it, and I ran upstairs and dressed in a hurry, afraid they would sell it for taxes. I rushed up to the tax office and paid that forty-eight cents before I had my dinner.

"Well, I built a house on that lot. I planned it and ordered every piece of lumber that went into it. The carpenters said, 'She is the stingiest girl—she has measured everything to the square inch and doesn't allow any waste.' I said, 'I don't mean to have any waste.' I was twenty-one or two then. I hired the carpenters by the day. You know how a house used to be built. I wanted a steep roof, and I built it with the idea that I would take the roof off and raise the house another story later on. I made a broad hall down the front. When I ordered the sheathing that's put on the rafters they said, 'Even to the sheathing she's calculated to the square foot,' and I said, 'I don't expect you to waste any.' They said, 'Suppose a piece splits?' 'Send it back and get a good one,' I said. When the logs were cut there would be a point, and they squared the lumber and there was a little scrap at the end. That wasn't counted in your bill. It was measured from where it measured square. They said, 'Maybe we'll have a wheelbarrow full of scraps.' I said, 'I'll throw it over the fence for Mother to burn in the stove.' Nothing was wasted . . .

"Well, I set those boxwood bushes in the ground—a sidewalk to the gate. I decided afterwards that I wouldn't leave them there—the carpenters had commenced tramping on them. I spaded them up and put them in a pile, and when I was married I took them over to Woodfin Street and set them out. After my first baby died and we got that burial lot out on the hill at Newton Academy, I set the boxwoods out there. When we moved my people and my baby, Leslie—and Mr. Wolfe's wife, Cynthia—when we moved them to this cemetery after Ben died, I moved these boxwoods too."

The rain was falling steadily now—not a warm spring rain, but chill.

"You'd better put this coat on, Mrs. Wolfe."

She shook her head.

"You'll catch cold, Mrs. Wolfe."

"You know, I always did like to work in the rain," she said. "Always liked to get out in the rain and work."

She went on presently to tell about Cynthia, whose body had been moved from Newton Academy cemetery at the time the boxwoods were moved.

"But that wasn't the first time she was moved," said Mrs. Wolfe. "They buried her first in the Methodist graveyard. Someone gave permission and someone else claimed it was their lot. So she was moved. The winter Mr. Wolfe and I were married, we had her moved out to the old Newton Academy graveyard. Mr. Wolfe didn't want her sent to Raleigh, where she was from. It wasn't sentiment—it was just the expense of taking her up and sending her all the way to Raleigh. And Father said, 'I'll tell you—we'll fence this lot in at Newton Academy and measure it off, half of it for your family and the other half for mine.'

"So we moved her. It came a cold spell in March, and the wind blew. Mr. Wolfe got three negroes—Jim and Dan Brown and old Uncle Prov—to go out to the Methodist graveyard and dig up this box. Mr. Wolfe's sister-in-law, Mary Wolfe, and Mrs. Bunn came over to the house that morning. Mrs. Bunn was a great friend of Cynthia's while she was sick. Mrs. Bunn said, 'We're going out to the Methodist graveyard to see them take it up.'

"But Mr. Wolfe said he wasn't going. He said, 'They know all about burying that box.' 'Well,' I said, 'I'm going—I hope when I die there will be some friend, somebody other than three negro men to see me put in my last resting place—and I'm going to see that they don't just put it down any old way. I'm going to see that it's done right.'

" 'Well,' he said, 'if you are determined to go, just wait till I put these tools away and I'll go with you.' And he laid aside his mallet and his chisel and we went on, and we met the negroes down where Church Street comes into Biltmore Avenue—an old horse and wagon don't go very fast—and Mrs. Bunn got up on that wagon and made those men open up that casket and open the lid and let her look in. She said, 'Oh, that red hair has filled the whole casket!'—Cynthia had red hair—Mr. Wolfe used to call her Reddy. But the brown silk dress she'd been buried in was just like it was.

"They closed the box and went on. It struck me queer that Mr. Wolfe showed no emotion. The vault wasn't long enough and they had to spend some time chipping it off, and the lid was always coming loose on the box, showing the casket inside. Mr. Wolfe noticed little bulges all over the top of the casket, and he took out his penknife and cut into one of them. He said, 'The damned scoundrels! I bought it for solid walnut, and here the veneer is rolling up. It's nothing but white pine!'

"Well, we walked around while the negroes worked, and we read the inscriptions on the old stones. On one of them it said, 'Here lies the first white child born west of the Blue Ridge.' It was windy, freezing, wait-

ing for them to finish with that grave—a wonder we
didn't catch pneumonia. They were about finished and
I said to old Uncle Prov, 'You see that everything is
cleared up, and we are going. I am hungry.' It was
nearly four o'clock and we walked on. Mr. Wolfe went
to his place of business and when he came home to
supper he had been drinking. He sat in the corner in his
dressing gown all next day, very pale. I gave him soft-
boiled eggs and made him coffee . . ."

The raindrops were larger now, and they pattered
whisperingly as they fell.

"Mrs. Wolfe," I said, "you'd better put on this coat."

She declined my offer with an outward thrust of her
hand. She turned to break a dead twig off a rosebush
and I slipped into the coat myself.

"I remember like yesterday the first time I saw Cynthia," she went on. "Mr. Wolfe married her, you know,
in Raleigh, and about six months after that she opened
a shop here in Asheville. She wasn't a very strong
woman, but she was a fine milliner. At that time I was
going to school at the old Female College. I went to
Mr. Pleasant's store and I asked, 'Have you got any
hats?' He said, 'They're hard to get, to tell the truth—
but there's a lady across the street putting up a milli-
nery store and she trims hats.'

"So I went across, and she was in there, and she had
boxes of things she had shipped in; she was opening
up at the beginning of the week, and she wanted to

know when I would want the hat. I said, 'Oh well, so I get it by Saturday.' Well, that's the way it was all right. I bought the first hat she sold in Asheville.

"Well, one day I stopped in, and she said, 'How are you, little Julia?' I wasn't large; I grew two or three inches after I was twenty-two, though. She told me she had been married six months, and she said, 'I got a letter from my old man today.' And I said, 'I bet he is an old man, too. You say you've been married only six months—and no young man would marry an old maid.'

"You see, she was thirty-six years old—a real old maid in those days. 'No,' she said, 'No, he isn't an old man.' 'What are you talking about,' I said, 'a young man marrying an old maid!' She says, 'No, he's a good looking man, and ten years younger than I am.' I said, 'Was he blind?' 'No.' 'Crazy then?' 'No.' 'What did he marry you for, then?' I asked. 'Well,' she said, 'he just found out he couldn't do without me. He boarded at my mother's house and I did his darning and patching, and he couldn't do without me.' 'Well,' I said, 'I wouldn't have married a man because he wanted me to patch for him.'

"And all that went through one ear and out the other. I was busy, you know, and studying; I was going to Hendersonville to school, and when I came back Cynthia had moved over onto College Street into another place, and I went in and she said, 'Little Julia, what can I do for you?' And I said, 'I came over to see how you looked in your new place.' And she said, 'Say, that old man you used to talk about—he's here—right back there.' And Mr. Wolfe was sitting back at the stove.

"Well, I had studied a book on phrenology, and Cynthia knew about it. I had learned a lot about the shape of people's heads, made quite a study of it, and Cynthia had said several times that I was right about their characteristics and so forth. So now she said, 'I want you to come here and phrenologize his head. I've been telling him about you, but he doesn't know how good you are.' Well, he looked like he was a little bit afraid. I didn't come near him. I said, 'Say, I can tell you all you want to know right now. He is the most selfish man you have ever had anything to do with.'

"And Cynthia screamed and hollered and clapped her hands, and he went out that back door, and she called, 'Come back, come back,' but he didn't come back. She laughed and laughed. The reason she got so excited was because I had made use of the very words she had always said about him—'The most selfish person I have ever met in my life.' And she thought that was the best thing, because he resented it.

"She did everything for him, though. She was in love with him way back before he knew anything about it, I think, and she would have given her life for him—that was the way she was. I said to him afterwards, 'She is the only one that ever did love you—what you call unselfish love—but you never appreciate the water until the well goes dry.' "

She paused and fingered a waxen leaf of the boxwood thoughtfully. I was thinking about crawling into the automobile out of the rain. But I knew I wasn't going to get into the automobile. After all!—a chap of thirty-four sitting in an automobile out of the wet while a woman in her eighty-third year worked on undismayed among the silent, glistening markers. I drew my chin lower into the collar of my coat, and water ran off the brim of my hat.

She pursed her lips, shook her head, a slight, abrupt movement, and smiled presently, looking at me with mischievously shining eyes.

"Mr. Wolfe was a good safe business man," she said. "He didn't believe in gambling. But he did that time . . . I'll tell you the story about that. I was one of those dread book agents at that time, after Mr. Wolfe's wife died. I had an agency; I took the orders during vacations and in the afternoons and Saturdays. I didn't go into all the business places. I was very particular. I was prissy, you know, didn't go just anywhere. I went into the tailor shop next door to Mr. Wolfe's place. It was Mr. Shartle's shop. He was a very fine man, and after he had bought a book I asked if any of his tailors might like to see my book. He said, oh no, they didn't read.

" 'But,' he said, 'You go in next door. Mr. Wolfe will

buy your book.' And I said, 'Do ladies go in there?' He laughed and said, 'You go in and tell him I said to buy this book.' So I went. I stood in the room outside his office. He was working on a stone, and I saw he had his apron on. I can see him now, throw that apron off and grab his coat when he saw me. I was pretending I didn't see him. When he opened the glass door I said, 'Don't get excited. I'm not a customer. I don't need a stone to-day.'

"And he was all smiles. I said, 'I am one of those dread book agents. Your neighbor sent me in here. I'm not going through the regular sales talk. I'll just show you the book and you can look through it and put your name down here.' Well, he thumbed through it and put his name down like I said. Then he asked me, 'Do you ever read novels?' 'Oh,' I said, 'I read most anything. Not the Bible as much as I should, though.'

"He said, 'I have a set of books; they are fine, too —love stories. Did you ever read "St. Elmo"?' 'No,' I said, 'but a friend of mine said he had the book and would bring it to me.' 'Well,' he said, 'I have it.' And he went on to say what a fine book it was. I said, 'I have got a prospectus coming—a book called "Thorns in the Flesh"—I'll bring that around. It's a historical novel of the Civil War.' He said, oh yes, he liked history. I thought, here's a customer before the book comes.

"Well, he sent a colored man with 'St. Elmo' for me to read. Two days after that I started out to sell

'Thorns in the Flesh.' It was a book that was written from the Southern point of view, but I didn't stop to think that Mr. Wolfe was from the North, a Yankee— I guess they called him a damn Yankee in Raleigh— but he changed his views and sided with the people in the South when he saw how they were treated in the Reconstruction Days. He was bitter against the North when he saw how they were treated.

"Well, I came across the Square to Mr. Wolfe's place of business. When I came across, the door was closed and I thought, 'He may not stay up here every day.' But I was bent on showing him that book because he said he was interested in history. I wasn't thinking about him being a Northerner, and of course, as I say, that book told the Southern side of it.

"Well, I knew where he lived on Woodfin Street. It was a little out of my way, but anyhow it was time to go home to dinner, nearly one o'clock, and I thought, 'I'll just go by there, and if he is home I'll show him the book.' He answered the door, and I told him that I was on my way home to dinner and I saw his shop door closed and didn't suppose he went up there every day, not thinking it was dinnertime for him, too.

"He said, 'We are at dinner; I'll tell Mrs. Allen.' Mrs. Allen was his mother-in-law, Cynthia's mother, and she lived there and took care of him, and he said, 'I'll tell Mrs. Allen,' and he called her and spoke to her. Of course, I know now that he was telling Mrs. Allen to make another place at dinner. They were about finished, and so she appeared at the door and said, 'Oh, how do you do?' She knew me; was already acquainted with me. She said, 'Come right on in. I've brought in a fresh bowl of soup.'

"I said, 'I was just going on home.' 'No, you come on in.' And Mr. Wolfe, he was the same way. I don't know whether I ate much or not, I talked so much. After we had finished, I said, 'I'll show you this book.' Mrs. Allen said, 'I'll come in the parlor just as soon as I put my things away and wash up the dishes.'

"Well, I went into the parlor and Mr. Wolfe showed me those old stereoscope pictures, you know, a lot of views made way back in Civil War days, the Battle of Gettysburg, the Blue and Gray lying around on the field. He would put in the slides while I looked at them. I said, 'I wish Mrs. Allen would come on in—I will have to go on home, and you, I suppose, want to go back to your business.'

"He said, 'Oh, my business doesn't amount to anything. I don't have to be up there.' He said, 'Mrs. Allen wants to go back to Raleigh to her people as soon as she can. She is just staying here because I hate to break up housekeeping. I've had a home for several years and I hate breaking up. I could sell the place, but I hate breaking up. But I will have to sell it or get married.'

"It never occurred to me that I was a marriageable girl, and I said, 'If you ever expect to get married again, I guess it would be the best thing to get married instead of breaking up the home.' 'Well,' he says, 'I think so, too.' He said, 'I have made up my mind.' He took my hand—I think he took my hand. He said, 'I have been looking at you for quite a while, looking at you as you passed, and I've had it in mind to ask you to marry me.'

" 'You don't know me,' I said. 'I've had one love affair three or four years ago, and since then I've made up my mind to stay an old maid.' 'No,' he said, 'that won't do. I want you to marry me. What's the answer?' And I said, 'Oh, let's look at the pictures.' Then I said, 'I've finished the book and I will return it. I didn't bring it today because I went down town.'

" 'Oh, that's all right,' he said. And he said, 'I've got another one—"Infelice." I'll let you read that, too.' 'Now,' I said, 'let's talk about the pictures.' 'No,' he said, 'let's talk about getting married.' I said, 'Oh, but I'm the old maid.' He said, 'I want to know what the answer is going to be.' He said, 'Give me some idea of what kind of answer it's to be.' I said, 'There's no answer. You don't know me, and I don't know you, only by sight.'

"He said, 'Well, we can learn.' So I said—well, you know, I had the book in my lap—I said, 'Well, I tell you, let's do this. You close your eyes and look away, and I'll open the book and on the right hand side, the middle of the page, the paragraph in the middle, whatever it says, we will abide by it.' He said, 'That's a gamble—I don't want to do that.' I said, 'I'm willing to abide by it. I don't know what's in this book, but I'm willing to do it.' It was just a piece of foolishness on my part, but Mr. Wolfe objected, said it was gambling.

"Well, you know, I opened that book—and what do you suppose I opened it to? When I opened it on that page, it said, 'Till death do us part.' It was a place in the story, I suppose, telling about a marriage. 'Oh,' he said, 'that's it, that's the very thing.' And I said, 'My finger must have slipped.' And he said, 'We're going to let it stand.' He claimed that fate had ruled that was the way it should be.

"Well, I thought he would forget about it. But he didn't. He was a widower, his wife not dead quite a year, and he was like all widowers. He didn't let the grass grow under his feet. He wanted to finish what he had started. I never did tell him that I would marry him. He took it for granted . . ."

"I think we'd better go, Mrs. Wolfe," I said. "It's more than a shower—it's turned into a steady rain."

She glanced at me sharply, plucked at her nose for a moment, leaving a smudge. Suddenly she smiled.

"My goodness, boy," she said, "you're all wet! Well, I tell you what—I'll take you home and hang you up to dry. Don't worry, you'll be all right. You'll be as good as new with some dry clothes on."

Chapter Two

I first met Mrs. Wolfe in May, 1941, when I drove to Spartanburg to visit a soldier friend at Camp Croft, and the name Asheville stopped my moving finger on the road map. With me on the trip were Mina, who later became my wife, and Hilda, my sister. They opened their eyes at me and exclaimed over my excitement.

Several hours later we drove into the Square at Asheville and in response to my inquiry at an information booth—I asked if any members of Thomas Wolfe's family still lived in the city—was told that his mother lived on Spruce Street.

Within a few minutes I stopped the car before the silent, decaying house on sloping Spruce Street. There was a sign hanging over the front steps, "Old Kentucky Home." I sat and looked and looked: this was Dixieland, the "bloody barn," Mrs. Gant's rooming house of "Look Homeward, Angel," and "Of Time and the River." There was the large, deep porch on which the boarders had rocked, awaiting dinner, while W. O. Gant held forth, squirting tobacco juice now and then into the flowers below. And within those walls—needing new paint—Gant had died of his cancer, and somewhere in there Ben, too, had died.

I could not bring myself to go to the door and knock. Wolfe had not written of his mother too kindly; Eliza Gant was not a completely amiable person. I had read that the name of Thomas Wolfe was anathema to Asheville after "Look Homeward, Angel" was published. Had not his mother, too, perhaps, cast him out? Was it not reasonable to expect her to slam the door upon my impertinence in knocking?

Suddenly I caught sight of the sign hung out—rooms. Strange that I had not seen it immediately.

"Go in," I urged Mina, "and see if we can get rooms to stay overnight. If I go in, she might see in my eyes —she might guess the real reason, and not let us stay."

At this point the front door opened and Mrs. Wolfe emerged with two carpenters and their tools. She had on a slatternly house dress and a sweater. There was a black skull-cap on her head. She came down the front steps, off the porch, deliberately, carefully, one step at a time. Knuckles on hips, she talked to the men. Occasionally she made vigorous masculine gestures with her hands. Apparently she was explaining to them about fixing the steps, and in a short time they began working.

Mina went up the cement steps—the lawn was above

the street level—and advanced up the cement path to the steps of the porch. Mrs. Wolfe, standing solid planted, watched the carpenters, and when Mina spoke to her, she turned, arms akimbo. Plucking at her nose several times, she listened to Mina's hurried story. She nodded and smiled and presently began explaining to Mina what the carpenters were doing. It was a minor job, one portion of the step had rotted dangerously. After a while she began showing Mina the flowers and I sat in the car pretending no interest at all. Mina returned to the car some half hour later. "We can stay there," she said.

"Tell her we'll be back later," I said.

"We'll be back later," Mina called.

"What say?" demanded Mrs. Wolfe.

"We'll be back later."

"Oh—all right—all right." It was a husky voice, old-mannish almost, tinged with southern-ness.

We drove away. I thought this might be a clever stunt, to appear not overly eager, to allay any suspicions Mrs. Wolfe might have about why we wanted to stop at the house.

I stopped to inquire of a boy the way to the cemetery where Thomas Wolfe lay. The lad did not know. I drove into a gas station and the attendant also professed complete ignorance. I wondered whether they really didn't know, or felt so bitterly about Wolfe that they held it taboo to talk of him.

When I slowed the automobile alongside a well-dressed, intelligent looking man, I inquired merely the way to the cemetery. He asked which one. I was by this time embarrassed and confused, and said, "Oh, any one."

He told me the way, and following his directions we came to a neglected burying-ground on the outskirts of Asheville. It looked just the place to bury a man who had nailed his neighbors in books, and we rushed from one weedy grave to another. But after three-quarters of an hour, we began to lose zest. Mina complained that the brambles had ruined her stockings.

So when a middle-aged couple entered the place and regarded us curiously, I squeezed up courage and inquired if Thomas Wolfe was buried here. The man, clerical and kindly, probably the minister of the church nearby, said Wolfe was buried on the other side of town. He told us how to get there. He said Wolfe had a handsome stone. He was so kindly, I inquired what the people of Asheville thought of Wolfe now. He replied that everyone had the greatest admiration for his writings, and I felt better. I inquired the way of half a dozen others before I finally drove the car around the curving unpaved road on which the Wolfe knoll abutted.

We were standing before the shining marker on which TOM was chiseled, when an elderly man drew near. "I see you're from out-of-state," he observed.

"Yes, they come from all over," he continued presently, "to see Tom Wolfe's grave—and the Angel."

He informed us that he was the sexton. He told of the gigantic casket they had put into the earth, so huge the removal of a tree had been necessary. "He was a big man," the sexton went on meditatively. "A giant. I used to see him. Every time he came to the cemetery, he went to see the Angel."

Eagerly I inquired regarding the whereabouts of the Angel, and he consented to show us the way. I invited him to ride with us—he said it was some little distance. "It faces east," he informed us, "Mecca, you know."

He had a fund of mortuary anecdotes. He told about a man who inquired concerning his plot on Saturday and was buried on Monday. Of Mrs. Wolfe he remarked, "Smart old lady—smart as a cricket." He showed us an angel and when we were ready to go I slipped a dollar into his hand.

After eating at a restaurant on the Square, we returned to the house on Spruce Street. We stood on the porch and in a few minutes Mrs. Wolfe appeared. Mina said to her, "Hayden's read all of your son's books—he admires them so much."

I stood looking down into the shrewd, observant features of the original Eliza Gant. With voice strained by emotion, I said, "Your son was a great man."

Her lips moved without parting. Suddenly her brown eyes shone wetly and she said, "Tom was a good boy

—a good boy. Say, did you know him?" she inquired, looking at me tensely. I said I hadn't, and she showed us the way down the high cheerless hallway.

On the gray wall, to the left, there were three angels framed, with the legend:

PEACE BE UNTO THIS HOUSE

There was a stove in the hall. The day was fine and warm, but the hall smelled of winter. In the rear of the hall, to the left, the wide stairway, cloaked in mouldy carpet, led to the upper chambers. I thought of young Thomas Wolfe going up and down the steps, fast, the way kids do. I thought of him grown to towering size, introspective, on these same steps. I thought of Ben. I thought of the activity on these steps the night Ben died.

Mrs. Wolfe led the way up. She told us there were a good many rooms vacant and it didn't matter which ones we slept in. The chambers were high and bare-looking. The walls were calcimined. The furniture was old-fashioned and few of the beds, bureaus and stands appeared to match.

The girls decided on a room, and I took one across the hall. I wondered which room had been Ben's. Mrs. Wolfe turned to me suddenly and said aggressively,

"Say, where did you go? Did you go to the cemetery?"

I was astonished that she had guessed correctly, and then remembered that the sexton said they all went to see the grave and the Angel.

"I wish you had told me you were going," his mother said. "I'd have gone with you."

"Would you like to come with us now?" I asked eagerly.

She said it was too late, the gates would be locked now. "But I tell you what," she said, "I'll go with you people tomorrow."

I told her that we had seen the Angel.

"Angel? What angel?" she asked, her expression sharp and suspicious.

"Why, the one your son wrote about," I mumbled. "The sexton showed us."

Her voice came out strong, husky and indignant. "Why, there's no such thing! That angel he showed you is not the one Tom wrote about. Tom's angel isn't in the cemetery. That man—I've spoken to him about it—he imposes on visitors. He shows them that old angel and tells them that it's the one, and then they give him money for tips."

"Where is the Angel, then?" I asked.

Mrs. Wolfe said she wasn't sure where it was. But she was sure it wasn't anywhere in Asheville's cemeteries. Some wealthy man bought it for his daughter, she said. It was so long ago that she didn't rightly recall to what nearby town it had been sent. She thought it might have been Hendersonville. She said she planned to go some day to the cemetery in Hendersonville to make sure.

"Then Queen Elizabeth didn't buy the Angel for one of her girls?" I asked.

"Oh no, Tom just changed things all around in the story," Mrs. Wolfe said. "But you speak of Queen Elizabeth, that reminds me . . ."

We were downstairs now, at the foot of the stairs, near the telephone attached to the wall. She jerked her hand in a masculine movement, "There's a wardrobe in the room here—it's walnut," she said. "I said to Tom one day, 'Here's something that brings back Queen Elizabeth.' Tom got it in the story that way, but it was Ella Chapman who came in to Mr. Wolfe one day. One of her girls had died over in the house she kept, and she bought her a grave space and a marker from Mr. Wolfe. She gave the name, and then he says, 'Do you want an inscription on it?' And she says, 'Just put requiescat in pace.' She said the girl who'd died was one of the best she had had. When Tom wrote the story he changed it to Queen Elizabeth. But it was Ella Chapman's girl. She was highly educated, but she'd run away from home and didn't want her people to know about it. Some of the Sunday school people went over there and sat up the night when she was so sick, and she told Mr. Rankin who she was, but didn't want to be sent back home, and she professed her religion and all. Mrs. Ella Chapman kept a house over in nigger town. It was licensed then."

"Wasn't there a real Queen Elizabeth?" I asked. "Or did Thomas make it up?"

"Oh, there was a girl called Evelyn something or other," replied Mrs. Wolfe. "She was a beautiful young woman, and she was so neat, and she rented a house and kept a young ladies' seminary, as the boys used to call it, down there, and she passed by Mr. Wolfe's place lots of times. He liked to stand out front and watch people pass when he wasn't busy. They would come up Eagle Street and come around that way.

"I was standing there with him one day and he said, 'There they go—two ladies dressed to kill!' I said, 'How could you tell who they are?' 'Oh,' he says, 'the way they are all painted up.' Nice girls then didn't paint. He said, 'They always paint up so the men will know them from everybody else.' This Queen Elizabeth used to pass there and he said she was a beautiful woman. All the men called her the queen because she carried herself so well and dressed well. She was so modest on the street, nothing bold about her.

"One day I was in at Smith's Drug Store with Mr. Wolfe, and he said, 'There's the Queen,' and I said, 'Who do you mean?' He said, 'Queen Elizabeth—she's over there buying toilet articles and everything.' She was very modest and beautifully dressed, cream-colored tailored suit, and a leghorn hat with yellow plumes. When she went out I said, 'She is certainly a nice look-ing woman,' and Mr. Wolfe said, 'All the men call her

Queen Elizabeth.' Tom knew the story later on in life . . .

"Well, this wardrobe in the room—it belonged to Ella Chapman, and Mr. Wolfe didn't have any closet in his room—just an improvised one. He went to old Mr. Moore in the second-hand furniture business, and he bought this wardrobe when Ella Chapman left here. Mr. Moore bought that wardrobe from Ella Chapman. Mr. Wolfe says, 'Well, I want that wardrobe to put my clothes in. You can send it down to the house.' And he told me, 'Well, I got Ella Chapman's wardrobe,' and I said, 'You wouldn't put your clothes in anything that came from Ella Chapman's would you?' And he said, 'Why not? She wore good clothes.'

"I guess I took my time cleaning that thing out— although it wasn't actually what you'd call dirty. He had it for his clothes. I have never had it for mine. . . Say, I found a heap of whiskey bottles in that wardrobe when those people left the other day. They had the room and said they couldn't afford to pay the price, but I found the bottles when they left.

"They didn't bother me very much. When they came here they said they couldn't afford to pay very much until they got started, and I said, 'I haven't rented that room for less than five dollars,' and they said they couldn't afford to pay more than three-fifty. They had to furnish their own coal. I guess sometimes it cost them two or three bags at fifty cents each for the week. I considered that all told it might have cost them a

dollar and half a week, and said, 'When you quit burning coal you'll have to pay me more.' Well, the last
time he paid me I told him, 'After this week I'll have
to have five dollars a week for that room.' I always
give people notice so that if they want to go, they can
go. He found a place in West Asheville."

I saw in the hall a marble door-stop, the top bearing
carved lettering:

J. E. W. from W. O. W. 1884

"Oh, yes," said Mrs. Wolfe, "he sent me that for a
Christmas present. Christmas morning he sent me the
door block and some handkerchiefs. He wrote a note,
said he understood I was going to get married. I hadn't
told him I was going to get married, but there was that
door block to put at the front door and that note, saying on second thought I might regret the step I had
taken and then I would need lots of handkerchiefs.

"In the sun parlor there is another door block with
'Reddy' cut on it," she continued. "I remember Dr.
Purefoy saw it and wanted to know what that was, and
Mr. Wolfe said he gave it to Mrs. Wolfe. He always
called her Reddy because her hair was red.

"Well, you know, I knew her about six months before Mr. Wolfe came up here, and I was away from
home and didn't see much of her after he came, and
they built down on Woodfin Street and lived here about
three years before she died. They had to build because

there wasn't any place to live. That was Asheville's condition then.

"You know, there are a lot of people that marry widowers and are bitter against the first wife. I had no bitterness. She was dead. I knew her living, but she had passed on. There's a woman who married Judge Moore—every time he turned the picture of his wife forward, she would turn it face to the wall, and finally he took the picture down. Wouldn't let the first wife hang there. I dare say it's all right—he should have put it away."

We sat on the porch in the rocking chairs and Mrs. Wolfe talked. Night fell. We bent toward her dim figure in the dusk, and her voice ran on, husky and animated. Three times that night her voice choked up and she wiped her eyes in the dark: when she told of the passing of Grover, of Ben, and of Thomas.

She said, "If only Tom had married . . . He said he would like to settle down . . ."

I inquired regarding the girl in "Look Homeward, Angel," Laura James.

"This girl Clara Paul was the Laura James in the book," Mrs. Wolfe said. "She came up here and made no secret she had her trousseau. Her little brother had had a sick spell, and she brought him up here, and I told Tom to go with them everywhere. I considered Tom a child. I don't suppose he was over fourteen or fifteen years old. I never thought about it. They went to Riverside Park—took trips to the mountains. The little boy went with them. I was perfectly honest in trying to treat a stranger well. She had said, 'If Tom will go, I'll pay his fare everywhere.'

"One day out on the porch, I went around the porch and Mabel was out there, and Clara and this little boy and Tom. Tom was sitting on the railing. Mabel said, 'Mama, did you know your baby has fallen in love?' I saw how red Tom's face had gone, and I said, 'Don't tease him, he isn't thinking anything about the girls.' Tom had often told Mabel, 'Mama never expects me to grow up. I'm just the baby.'

"Well, I never thought about Mabel talking about him falling in love with Clara. Clara was to be married in two weeks after she left here. She went to Norfolk to live, and she died, but I don't know when. Somebody told Tom. He never saw her in Norfolk, though he passed the house a time or two.

"It was just a fascination. He knew she was going to be married at that time. She was ready. She brought the boy up here, this little boy . . . I don't know where her husband-to-be was. She was a fairly good looking girl.

"Tom built it all up in imagination. He tells about Mabel fixing up a lunch for them. I remember, the little boy must have been nine or ten years old. Tom left him out of the book . . .

"It would have been so much better for Tom if he had found somebody later on in life—maybe he wouldn't have taken such an awful trip west. But fate's a queer thing. Works tragedy and tricks us all. He was tired when he took that trip west. He traveled about ten thousand miles. When he joined up with Harper's he said he was going to show them what he could do if it killed him, and he stuck right to it, but it killed him in the end. It seems like a tragedy all the way through —just put his time in writing. Maybe stayed too much in his rooms."

That night when I went to bed in the tall, gaunt chamber, and at last was drifting to sleep, I thought there came a slight creaking. In the dim light I saw Mrs. Wolfe drawing near the bed, ghostlike. She had an extra blanket and drew it over me, and in the morning I half thought it had been a dream.

We went out to the restaurant for breakfast and when we returned to the house, Mrs. Wolfe emerged from her room at the bottom end of the hall. Gone was the shabby dress and sweater. She wore black, a veil and gloves. Her eyes snapped. She was in a fine humor.

Mina suggested stopping at a florist's and Mrs. Wolfe directed the way to one that would be open this Sunday morning. Mina bought a potted plant, but Mrs. Wolfe wandered about the shop expressing dissatisfaction with the prices. Finally she selected a plant and commenced haggling with the clerk about the price. She pointed out a broken sprig. But the clerk was adamant and finally moved away. Mrs. Wolfe grumbled, but at last capitulated, going carefully into her purse.

At the cemetery Mina placed her plant upon Thomas Wolfe's grave. Mrs. Wolfe placed hers upon Mr. Wolfe's grave. But first she put the broken sprig into her purse, commenting that she might be able to slip it. "Things grow for me," she said. "You know, there's a verse in Proverbs that's mine: 'She considereth a field, and buyeth it: with the fruit of her hands she planteth vineyard.' "

She conducted us on a tour of the markers, both in the Wolfe plot and in the plot adjacent where the Westalls, her family, lay buried. She paused contemplatively before a low marker bearing the inscription:

JULIA E. WOLFE
NEE WESTALL
FEB. 16, 1860

"Most people," she said, "never get any good out of their stones. But I've got a lot of use out of mine. Many's the time I've come here and sat on it, and it's nice and comfortable, too."

She showed us a flat worn stone in the rear of the Wolfe monuments. The inscription read:

C. C. WOLFE
NEE HILL
SEPT. 18, 1842
FEB. 22, 1884

"Cynthia," she said. She regarded the marker meditatively, shook her head abruptly, frowningly. In a moment she dismissed the memory, whatever it was.

"Mr. Wolfe," she said, "went to Raleigh in the Reconstruction days—those days the South was bitter against the North and the North against the South. He was a Yankee, I expect they called him a damn Yankee. He married a Raleigh girl and they separated. She came from the society crowd. They had trouble right away. He was brought up in Pennsylvania where they had big feet, and he didn't know how to dance, and he married this girl—why, she went to dances about four nights out of every week.

"He couldn't dance and he didn't go, and some of her old boy friends came and took her to those dances. Of course, that didn't last long. They separated and she went back home. He got a divorce. There was the bitterness. A Yankee had come down there and it was a disgrace to be divorced. The whole town and neighborhood howled about it. He was in business there and it hindered him.

"Well, he boarded at Mrs. Allen's where Miss Cynthia was. Mrs. Allen had married for the second time, Old Colonel Allen. Some friend of Mr. Wolfe's told him to go over and board there, and they took him in. Miss Cynthia, of course, after he had been married and divorced, she took him in and her friends were bitter against her. He was prosperous, but all that went to help the lawyers out in the divorce trial, and finally his business went. The sheriff closed it up.

"He had nerve enough in that way—he got back on his feet again and married Cynthia Hill. She came up here to Asheville about six months afterwards and told him, 'Now, you leave there and sell out your things.' He wanted to stay in Raleigh—he wanted to reinstate himself. All those old people years later would come up here, the old aristocrats, lots of Raleigh people. They never forgot Mr. Wolfe, they all knew him. He never changed much in looks. They told him he looked like he always looked.

"Well, there was pride. The reason he wanted Effie to go to St. Mary's—he knew St. Mary's was patronized by the rich class, and he wanted to send his daughter down to Raleigh to St. Mary's to let those people know he could afford to send her there."

"How did Cynthia look?" asked Mina. "Was she pretty?"

"No, not pretty," replied Mrs. Wolfe. "Not pretty at all. She was old for her years."

"Did she have a nice personality?"

"Oh yes—and a good figure."

"What color eyes did she have?"

"Kind of gray . . . Say, what do you know—about those divorce papers now. Mr. Wolfe said, 'You know, I was married to Cynthia. But that wasn't the first time. I was married before that and divorced. I didn't want to marry you without telling you about it.' Well, you know there is something spooky about those divorce papers.

"I suppose we had been married maybe a year or more. Down in our living room there was a dresser with deep drawers, and in there was a box, a square wooden box, a letter box that you could lock. Well, it wasn't locked, but it was in the end of that drawer, and I didn't have enough curiosity to go ahead and read those papers.

"One day I said, 'Mr. Wolfe, we need that drawer— we could put things in it. What's the use of keeping that box of old letters and things? Why don't you destroy them?' He said all right, and he took that box out Sunday night and said, 'Well, there's the old divorce proceedings.' It wasn't typed—they didn't have typewriters then—it was all written.

"I said, 'What are you keeping them for?' He said, 'Oh, I don't know. It's just that I never got around to destroying them.' Well, we separated what we thought was any use keeping. It was Sunday night and we didn't have any fire in the stove. I put them in the stove, said, 'Well, that will be good to kindle the fire with in the morning.' It filled the whole fire box, that bundle.

"I dreamed that night I saw Mr. Wolfe sit up in the bed, and he said, 'She'll think it's burnt, if I take it out.' And I said to myself, 'If that isn't a trick!'

"Well, the next morning I slipped in there and said, 'I'll take it out myself. Maybe the papers oughtn't to be burned.'

"And the thing wasn't in there. I took everything out, and the papers weren't there. He came in, and I said, 'I dreamed you got the papers out, and I was going to save them and maybe I'd read them before I burned them, but they aren't there.' Mr. Wolfe said, 'Well, you search and see if you can find them. Do you reckon I could have gotten up in my sleep and put them away somewhere?' We searched the house, but we never did find them."

Mrs. Wolfe went on to tell how she had planned to have "mother of eight children" cut on her own stone, so that visitors would know Cynthia hadn't borne Mr. Wolfe any of the children. "All they'll have to do is count the stones," she said, "to see Cynthia didn't have any."

She said this quite matter-of-factly, without a shade of malice, and a few moments later stood over the small stone:

LESLIE E. WOLFE

OCT. 18, 1885

JULY 14, 1886

"She was my first baby. She died of cholera infantum, the doctor said, but it was only the poisoned cow's milk. Cholera infantum is what Dr. Clendenning calls acidosis, and that's nothing to do with bad milk. But old Dr. Nelson called it cholera infantum.

"I got the milk from the next door neighbor. Leslie

40

was brought up on cow's milk, and about six weeks before she died, the daughter came up with that long drawl of hers and she says, 'Miss Julia, papa sold the cow.' I said, 'Oh, my baby will die.' And she said, 'We're getting another one in the morning, a jersey cow.' And I said, 'But that baby was brought up on that other cow's milk.' You see, I had found that if they ran out of milk the baby got sick when I went somewhere to stay all day.

"Leslie was the healthiest child. Bishop Atkins lived up there and he came in to see the baby, and he said, 'Oh, I wish I could see this baby when it grows up! He thought she was so pretty . . .

"Before I was married, I was an agent for all sorts of books and pictures, and they sent me a kind of oilograph, taken from a great painting. It looked like an oil painting, a picture of one of the most beautiful children—she had the prettiest yellow curls and most angelic expression. Everybody who came in said, 'Oh, where in the world did you get that beautiful child?' And I said, 'That is my pattern.' And Leslie was modeled on the idea of that picture I kept set up on the mantle.

"Leslie was the whitest child I ever saw. She had pink lips and the prettiest blue eyes and light hair. Mrs. Ramseur dressed the child and brought her to me. She was a nice old lady, a friend of Mr. Wolfe's who came from down in the country. She delighted in dressing little babies, and I heard her say—she held it up this way—she said, 'Me's a white child. None of your little old red ugly babies. Me's a lady.'

"She brought her over to the bed for me to see, and she was looking all round with her blue eyes. She was the brightest baby. I saw she was superior to other people's babies, and because she was my baby I expected she would be better than any one else's. She never cried. She was so strong. You can't tell me babies don't know things.

"When she was three months old she would take hold of your finger this way—and you could hold her up and she would cling to your finger. Mr. Wolfe said, 'She's like a little hawk.' I said, 'Oh, you'll make her bowlegged, letting her stand like that.' And he would take her and say, 'Smart girl!' And she would laugh and look around to see if people would look at her.

"Mr. Wolfe was the happiest man in the world. But right here I can tell you that all men are really jealous after the children come. They think that the wife gives the children more attention than they do them, and they resent it. He used to say, 'You will do everything for the children; you don't think about me any more. I ought to come first—I was here first.' I said, 'You can take care of yourself. They are dependent.' But he was right, I suppose—though in another way he wasn't. The boys were all able to take care of themselves later on, and I would often do things for them. He came into the kitchen one day where I had been, and I had gathered up a lot of their shirts and laundered them, and had them all ironed, and he saw them. 'Yes, they throw their money away and you stand here and wash for them. I send mine to the laundry,' he said. I said, 'You have got your own money.' He said, 'They are making their own money, too.' I said, 'They don't have as much as you, and they want money to spend for other things.' But he resented it. He didn't like all that attention to the children. He was jealous. But most mothers are in love more with their children than they are with their husbands, after all . . ."

She felt of her nose, looking thoughtful. In a moment she spoke again of Leslie:

"Long before she died—she couldn't talk—but she could take that baby carriage and roll it all the way around the front porch. She would jabber and say, 'Ma-ma-ma-ma-ma.' She was trying to say mamma. She was so good you could put her down on the back porch and give her papers to play with, and she would never tear the papers. If you put her out in the yard, she would crawl up and pull the nasturtiums, but she would not touch anything else. She would hold a nasturtium in her hand until she withered the stem. She would sit in that baby carriage and wave her handkerchief at people passing on the street and smile at them. There was a girl from Detroit at Mrs. Israel's—their upper porch was just about level with our porch—and this Jones girl would call, 'Leslie,' and that baby would say, 'Huh.' She smiled at everybody, even the colored people who came around to be hired. She held up her hands

for them to take her, and smiled. It would tickle them
to death. She wasn't afraid of anybody. There were
some people here that summer who came and I rented
them a room. They boarded with me. They would say,
'Baby, why don't you cry. We don't know there is a
baby in the house.' I compared her with the others
when they came—Effie was the next one—but I said,
'She isn't bright like Leslie.' "

Mrs. Wolfe shuddered and her voice came out husky
and vibrant with doom: "The milk from that other cow
they bought just poisoned her. I tried to think she
would get used to it—that she was going to get along
all right. But that awful milk—I called to Mrs. Israel,
'Oh, Mrs. Israel, there's something wrong with the
milk!' And she said, 'We couldn't use it for breakfast.
The cook got sick and went home.' And it made the
child sick—why, it came up and it looked like sticks of
macaroni out of that child's throat when it came up.
Her eyes looked so large—I screamed when I saw it. I
sent for old Dr. Nelson, and I always have thought he
gave her too much paragoric . . . She only lived three
days.

"I thought the end of the world had come when
Leslie died. I remember Miss Emily Cole—she was
from New York—she said, 'That child's gone, and you
must forget it.' She was just an old maid."

She moved across the path to the Westall plot. The
graves here were somewhat unkempt, the stones not as
impressive as those in the Wolfe plot. For some mo-

ments she stood there musing. She spoke of her father:

"Way back there Father was a Presbyterian. There were so many young converts that he took it upon himself to teach them the confession of faith—and then he began to change. It changed his religion. Father was, well, I don't know what they would call it—so honest in every way. When he found he couldn't believe anything he would make a report.

"So he stopped teaching and went to the Presbyterians and told them he could not believe their religion any longer—that the confession of faith taught him things he had never realized before. And he resigned from the church. The confession of faith—the old confession of faith is pre-destination, that people born into the world are pre-destined to go into eternal punishment no matter what they do, and Father, he couldn't believe that, but Dr. Eller believed it and preached it a thousand times. About infants in hell a span long, and he said, 'It's your duty to go to church whether you believe in it or not. It's your duty to remain in the church.'

"But Father resigned. Well, all those ministers came here—they were leading people in the county, Dr. Chapman and Dr. Eller—and Dr. Eller really became —oh, he was fierce, you know, said, 'It's your duty to go to church.' I was only a child or girl, and I leaned out a window that was over the porch. Dr. Chapman was a fine old man, and he said, 'Brother Eller, don't be so severe.' But Dr. Eller said he believed in babes burning in fire, and Father left the church. Father was a great influence at Piney Grove and when he left, Uncle Bob Patton and Mr. Alexander withdrew, too.

"Well, you know, they made a report that was a terrible thing—somebody wrote it up in the Presbyterian paper in Wilmington, North Carolina, that T. C. Westall, Robert Patton and William Alexander were dismissed from the church for unchristian conduct and heresy. That's what was in the paper. But oh, didn't they get it! Father was a great writer, and he wrote the whole thing up. He made public just exactly what they didn't want him to make public—why he couldn't believe in the confession of faith—and they had to take it all back in the next report . . .

"Father was a very fine man. None of his children took after him. Tom was the only one that took after him in writing. Tom was named after him. You know, Father never had the opportunity of college education —he was a self-educated man, but you wouldn't find a grammatical error of any description in any of his writings. That's more than you can say of any of his children, because they all make mistakes.

"I used to say he was born two hundred years before his time. None of his children measured up to him. Henry was scholarly, of course. In a way, Henry was a fine student and highly educated. But Father helped him out when he was a boy, you know—and I don't feel that Henry was the well-balanced man that Father was. Father was a different temperament, of course."

She shook her head, turning over her memories. Suddenly she looked at me keenly. "There was another principle Father had," she said. "He was a teetotaler, a temperance lecturer. Father never knew the taste of alcohol. He was the editor of a temperance paper. Well, he worked hard to put down whiskey, but never lived to see it voted out.

"He was a contractor and builder, and after he couldn't do that any longer, Captain M. E. Carter who was a great friend of Father's—a younger man, he had this internal revenue job and had to employ people— he said, when I was up there, not for anything of that kind, but Captain Carter was on a note and I wanted to collect some money—and he said, 'I just wish I had your father up here.'

"It was before they had typewriters, and he knew Father could write such a plain hand, just like script —don't know why his children didn't take after him. And he said, 'I wish I could get your father up here.' I said, 'Why don't you ask him?' And he said, 'You ask him for me.' So I went to Father and said, 'Father, I have got a job for you. It's easy—just something you would like—figuring and writing.' And I told him where the work was.

"He said, 'Why didn't he ask me? He knows better than to ask me.' I didn't see the point, and he said, 'I have fought whiskey all my life—could I accept a salary drawn from the taxes on whiskey and tobacco? I have a principle, and Captain Carter didn't ask me himself because he was afraid I'd send it right back to him that he ought to have more principle than be engaged as a collector in such a business.'

"Well, I said, 'Father, I don't know—somebody is going to get that money, and you can't put the whiskey out, no matter if you don't believe in it.' But he said, 'No, I wouldn't take a salary off it, against my principle.' That was queer, wasn't it?"

She shrugged, her hands clasped before her, and looked at the graves. Presently she bent to pluck out a weed.

After a while we returned to the house on Spruce Street. Mrs. Wolfe brought out pictures, faded family groups of the whole Wolfe family and sleek professional ones of Thomas done in New York City. There was one of Mr. Wolfe standing before his tombstone shop, one of Thomas in college, hundreds of others. We sat on the front steps and listened to her running commentary as she passed them around. She went into the house and brought out a big volume badly in need of rebinding, entitled "Golden Treasury of Poetry and Prose," edited by R. H. Stoddard and F. F. Browne, 1883.

"I bought that book," she explained. "Tom and Mr. Wolfe wore it out. You know, Mr. Wolfe had a remarkable memory of things, if he learned them. Now, Grey's Elegy, he would recite that. Shakespeare, any old place or anything. Oh, a remarkable memory—even when he was sick in that room in there. There was an old Englishman came here—his name was Burtwhistle. In the summertime I told him he would have to get him another place, and he would recite from memory, you know. I told Mr. Wolfe one day, 'The old man can recite things, but he hasn't anything on you.' And Mr. Wolfe started to recite the 'Bridge of Sighs,' and I said, 'The old man has a remarkable memory, but not ahead of you that way.'

"Yes, he would often recite passages from most anything if there was something that reminded him, that he could apply. He would take passages and apply them to most anything that occurred. And a nice strong voice, you know. He would go to the phone to call up somebody, and I would say, 'Why don't you go out on the porch, they can hear you from there!'

"He talked so loud and everybody sat and listened. I would be in the kitchen, and we would have boarders, and Mr. Wolfe would get talking about things on the phone and you couldn't hear anybody else. He would take a trip and see more on his trip, paint it up, tell everything. That California trip, he liked it, and the climate, and I would say, 'This dinner's not ready yet —go out on the porch, and to keep them from thinking the time's long, entertain them with your California trip and they'll forget.' Oh, they enjoyed it. Miss Hill was a retired teacher from New York—Mr. Wolfe had told her everything about California, and later she went there herself, all buoyed up about her trip. But after she had been out there for some time she wrote him a letter, said it was the most disappointing place she had ever been in, and she wrote, 'I can't understand why you would praise this climate, I can't go out without an umbrella or raincoat, it's so miserable.' Well, Mr. Wolfe looked around and said, 'Why, the woman talks like she thought I was lying. That was the way it was when I was there.' "

Mrs. Wolfe picked up a photo. "Here's Tom with two of them. The women were always trying to get near him. It was on the trip west . . ."

It was mid-afternoon and we had to be starting on our trip back to Pennsylvania. A complacent-looking, middle-aged gentleman came up the cement walk and looked at us mildly as we sat on the steps. Mrs. Wolfe introduced him, Elmer Westall, her brother.

He sat down and in a few minutes began to talk, the mild anecdotes of a well-bred small-town raconteur. I studied him for the Pentland characteristics Thomas Wolfe said were common to the family. He had the fleshy nose, broad at the wings. He bore a slight resemblance perhaps to his great nephew. He was glib, soft-spoken and not at all aggressive. I thought I saw a harried expression in his shy and yet sly-looking brown eyes. He told his sister that he had seen a copy of the latest *Life* magazine, that the pictures hadn't appeared yet.

Mrs. Wolfe told, then, about the *Life* photographer who had taken shots of her and of various scenes about the place and in Asheville. She said, "Elmer looks in *Life* every week—he can't wait to see how the pictures look."

A few minutes later we got up to go. Mrs. Wolfe shook hands all around. She gave me a firm grip and looked at me earnestly. She said, "I know I'll see *you* again."

Chapter Three

I wrote Mrs. Wolfe in January, 1942, asking permission to pay her a visit and perhaps gather material for a book on her. She replied—in one of her crowded, closely written letters—that I was quite welcome to come on down to Asheville. She said if I wanted to tackle a biography of her, she was willing—but that it might turn out a pretty big job, because she had lived so long and remembered so much.

So in early April, with sufficient funds to tide me over a few weeks, I drove to Asheville. It was one of those prematurely warm days when I arrived and there was a sweet smell of budding earth in the air. When I stopped the car before No. 48 Spruce Street, I saw Mrs. Wolfe near the side of the house, bending down and cleaning away last season's dead husks.

With a bag in one hand and my portable in the other, I went up and stood right behind her before she knew anyone was there. She gave a little gutteral exclamation and blinked at me in astonishment, but almost immediately smiled and reached out a dusty hand.

"Say, where did you come from?" she demanded. "You know, you wrote me, and I was expecting you—

but I wasn't thinking of you this minute, and then there you are standing here. How did you get here?"

"I drove down," I said, "in the automobile."

"Say, now, that's what I'd like to do," she said. "Just drive around the country and not have to do any work. Just pack up my bag and go."

She scrutinized me closely. "Where's Mina and your sister? Working?" She spoke in bantering manner: "Well, that's what I'd like—just be able to pack my things and drive around the country and not think about work. It's like the time I said to Tom that I'd like nothing better than some nice easy work like writing, and he put it in the story . . . You just got here, you say? You must be tired, all that driving. How long did it take? When did you start?"

She insisted on carrying the portable, and we went up the steps, into the hall where one was cut off immediately from the warm day. Carrying the typewriter, she mounted the carpeted stairs, one step at a time, talking meanwhile.

She showed me into one of the chambers. "I guess this will do—if you want another, just speak up. There's plenty of room, only one man here now and I don't see much of him."

I looked around the bare-looking, gaunt chamber. I hesitated, then said, "Mrs. Wolfe—where did Ben die?"

She looked at me, a strange, quick and penetrating look such as one sometimes notes in animals, not cats, but dark-eyed animals.

53

"Why, Ben's room—it's that one over there across the hall. The door's closed . . ."

She was silent a moment, her hands clasped before her.

"I was thinking of it the other day . . . That afternoon before he died—and in my mind, you know, I heard that song they were singing then—they sang it the night before he died, 'Just a Baby's Prayer at Twilight.' Well, that afternoon, he made one speech after another—wonderful speeches—but of course, I was so excited and worried because I knew he would wear himself out.

"Ollie Wolfe, his cousin, was here then, and he would say, 'Ben, Ben, somebody's asleep in the next room.' "

She spoke in a hushed, husky voice:

"I said to Ollie, 'Where in the world does he get all that? I didn't know he knew things like that.' And Ollie said, 'It's his subconscious mind.' And I said, 'Your subconscious mind must be far greater than your conscious mind.'

"I can't understand it—why, that boy went on to say there was a wonderful invention, a machine that could farm over the hills and mountains, oh a great help to the farmers, because all these tractors and everything work on level ground, but it's pretty hard on these mountains. You go out, way out by the Nantahala River, and they can't plow on those hills. A man can plant an apple orchard, but he has to dig out a platform before he can plant a tree. But this great invention, he said it would be a great benefit to the mountain farmers. Of course, Ben read a great deal, but he never said much about anything. If I had had somebody to take down what he said then, we would have it. I might have remembered it if I hadn't been so distressed.

"He just lay there in the bed and repeated those speeches. Ollie would call to him, 'Ben, Ben, don't talk so much.' I said, 'Oh, he'll wear himself out.' He would wait a second, and then commence again. He had the flu and I guess it was pneumonia and all. I sat there by his bed feeling his pulse and his heart beat. The last word he said, two or three hours before his breath left him—I had hold of his hand, and he said, 'Mamma— Mabel . . .' "

She clenched her mouth firmly, shook her head with a shuddering movement. She said:

"There was a Wolfe look more in Ben than any of the others. When he was a year or two old he looked like Mr. Wolfe's brother, Wesley. I'll show you his picture . . ."

And she did, that afternoon, in the chilly, bleak and arid parlor. I held the studio portrait in my hands and looked at the face of a lad perhaps in his early twenties: a good face, serious, yet humorous in a wry way; the features narrow and delicate, the light eyes clear and scornful and gentle.

On the wall there hung a large old-fashioned picture of Thomas Wolfe as a youngster, with long curls.

"There was something between Ben and Tom," the

mother said. "Something between them from the time
Tom was a baby that I never could explain. Tom
wanted me of course to stay with him if he was sick,
but I had so many things to do and I knew the others
could stay with him. So I had the children tend him,
and he would scream if one of them came about. So I
got Ben, and I found out that Ben could manage him
all right when he was a baby only a year or more old.
He didn't resent Ben, and that was the beginning of the
connection between the two.

"If Frank or Grover came near him, I would say,
'Come here and shake this carriage,' and he would just
scream. But Ben managed him. Of course after that
Ben would be called on to look after him if I had to
leave him.

"Ben was very gentle. Tom grew tall for his years
and I went down to M. V. Moore's and bought him a
nice suit and he looked so well in that suit, but I said,
'You must wear your other clothes every day and save
these.' Effie had asked me to let him come down to
spend Christmas with them, and the night before he
was to go I said, 'Ben, dress him up in his new suit and
see how nice he looks.' He had a new tie and shirt and
all. He went across in that front room—Tom was still
my baby, you know. He said years afterwards, 'Mamma
thought I never would grow up, and she was determined that I should sleep in that same room.' Well,
Ben dressed him up, you know. So prissy. I said, 'Don't
he look fine—but he looks like a grown-up boy now.

Where's my baby?' He said, 'Don't be foolish.' But I said, 'He is the last one of the family.'

"He was handsome in that suit, Tom was. I said, 'Fred Gambrell will know how to put that tie on, and you dress up in that suit Christmas day and have Fred tie your tie and fix you up nice.' The shirt was made with a collar to it . . . Well, when he came home, we could not get him out of those clothes. I said, 'I don't want you to wear them every day, and I can't buy another suit. Why,' I said, 'you have the other suit I bought that time in Baltimore—what are we going to do with the other suit?' And he said, 'Oh, get me some long pants and I can wear the coat.' So I had to go downtown and get the pants so he would wear the coat to school . . . No longer a baby any more.

"Ben took so much pride in dressing him up. I suppose Ben was right about it . . . Ben had bought a pair of shoes for himself, and I suppose had gotten them too tight. I said, 'Give them to Tom.' Tom thought maybe he would wear them, but they were too small for him, hurt his toes. Ben said, 'Mamma, for God's sake go and buy him a pair of shoes. His foot is as big as mine.'

"Ben fussed because I let Tom wear the shoes. He said, 'You go and buy him a pair.' That was before he went off to school, of course . . . I know Tom would have liked to have had the shoes because they were nice shoes, but they were too small.

"I have a letter where Ben went to Winston-Salem

shortly after Tom went to Chapel Hill. Easter Sunday
Ben had him come over to Winston-Salem, and they
got up to see the Moravian Easter, which is a wonderful time, and they got up at 12 o'clock at night. The
services are in the early morning at daylight, and with
all the flowers it is wonderful. People come in to see it,
thousands of them. Well, Tom enjoyed it so much—
and Ben had given him this nice time . . ."

She stood reflecting. She said, "They were all in love
with Ben . . . I think Ben really cared for Louise until he found out she didn't care for him, and she married a tobacco buyer who had more money than she
thought Ben would ever have . . . Well, all the way
back there—I don't remember who examined Ben for
the army. I suppose he was examined down at Winston-
Salem. He told me he had been turned down. He asked
me, 'Say, Mamma,' he asked me, 'the doctor asked me
if I ever had any kind of sweats or any hemorrhages.'
I could see he was worried about it, and I said I guessed
it was just a routine question, like they asked Mr.
Wolfe all kinds of questions before he was operated on.
Ben said he usually ran a little temperature. He smoked
too many cigarettes. At times he would have a cigarette
cough. But he must have gained ten pounds before that
flu broke out. Dr. Colby, the last day when Ben was
sick, he came in this room here, he said, 'No human being can save Ben's life.' I don't know—he had been
gaining weight . . ."

She saw me looking at the old-fashioned portrait of

a man with glaring eyes and drooping sandy moustache.

"Mr. Wolfe?" I asked.

"He is about thirty-five years old in that picture," she said. "I don't think he was really handsome then but he dressed well and kept himself looking all right. The women all liked him—liked him better than they did me. He was regarded as a highly eligible man. That picture is damaged. When we left Woodfin Street I packed them all in a box lined with zinc, and they brought them up here and put them in the basement. I was so busy that summer, I placed the furniture, but didn't have time for the pictures and when I did get to it, there were several of them kind of damaged . . .

"He was from Pennsylvania, raised in Pennsylvania. I was thinking of it this morning, the kraut he learned how to make when he was young . . . You know, I said it took me half the time putting away the food when I ought to have been doing something else. He was a good buyer and a good provider. They didn't have trucks then, and farmers used to come in with wagon-loads of things, and they stood down on the wagon lot, and one day this man said, 'Mr. Wolfe, I wish you would buy my load of stuff. I want to go back home tonight, and I can't leave my wagon here.'

Mr. Wolfe went there and looked it over and said it was entirely too much; why, he couldn't possibly use all that. But the man kept on at him, and Mr. Wolfe finally made him an offer, and it brought the price down. It was getting dark when he brought the wagon up the alley, and Mr. Wolfe was ahead of him showing him the way. And there were twenty-eight chickens. And more than a hundred heads of cabbage in that wagon. And potatoes. And hams. I don't know what all he didn't have.

"I said, 'Mr. Wolfe, what in the world did you get all that stuff for?' He said, 'The man wanted to go back and I offered him a cent a head for the cabbages and ten cents apiece for the chickens.' And I said, 'Aren't you ashamed?' And he said, 'I didn't want them—I told him I didn't, but he kept on after me, and finally I made him an offer.' I said, 'Oh, what are we going to do with all that cabbage?' I said, 'We can keep the chickens and eat them after a while—but all that cabbage!' And he said, 'We'll make some kraut, I guess.' I said, 'Yes, that's the thing—we'll just chop the cabbage and put it in some of those big stone jars.' Well, he didn't want to waste anything, either, and we made the kraut."

She glanced at the portrait briefly, plucked thoughtfully at her lips. "Everybody used to like Mr. Wolfe's work," she said. "The worst competitors he had would be some of these agents coming into town—you know, lots of people have a perfect mania for buying from an agent. Some of them would send clear up to Chicago to Sears Roebuck and get a piece of stone, and it would come lettered wrong, and they would send for Mr. Wolfe to fix it for them.

"Well, he would say, 'Send it back to Sears Roebuck

and let them letter it right. If you had bought it from me, it would have been lettered right, but I'm not doing any of Sears Roebuck's work over.'

"He was very conscientious with his work. Often when he put a stone up—he hated to see it discolored —but people would complain about the stone turning dark, and he would say it was the dripping off the trees. You know, oak stains. The rain dripping off the oak trees onto the white marble turns it black after a while. It doesn't stain granite as bad. Mr. Wolfe thought the cemeteries oughtn't to have oak trees in them. Spruce, pine and shrubbery were all right. Why, you can dye goods with the oak bark . . .

"But he was willing enough to clean the stones for people, if he got paid for it. He would have the darkey do it . . . You can clean marble with muriatic acid. He always kept muriatic acid, and I know I used to tell him after the children were born, 'You put that acid where they can't get to it.'

"He would lay off the letters on stone offhand, he had done so much, had so much practice. He would take the inscription and pencil it all off, maybe chisel around a little bit. I had seen him cut letters so often —one day he was sick in bed and this man from the country came to get his stone, and I said, 'It's about finished, I'll go up there and see.' The man had come all the way, maybe fifteen or twenty miles in an old wagon.

"Well, the stone was on the block. I saw the lower

part, the epitaph on the bottom, kind of blocked out. I thought, 'That will never do.' So I said to the man, 'You have some business to attend to, haven't you? I'll fix this stone for you—it needs a little cleaning up.' I took those chisels and finished it—never had cut a letter in my life. And the man came back and said it was all right. I told Mr. Wolfe about it afterwards . . .

"He took Ben up there, you know, for a while. Ben wasn't with the paper at the time. I said, 'Ben, if you want to go in and learn to letter and sell, it's all right. I'll make him turn over half the business to you.' Ben went up, but he didn't stay more than a week until he told me, 'I'm not going to work up there unless he pays me a price.' Mr. Wolfe would have liked Ben for the work because Ben was very particular. But I told Ben, 'I wouldn't work unless he paid me a salary. You can't take an interest in anything without that.' I never did tell Mr. Wolfe."

"Did Mr. Wolfe die in this house?" I asked.

"Yes . . . In the summertime he occupied the room on the back porch. It was near where I could go back and forth. Nice large room, too. We never did tell him it was cancer. He said, 'If you're going to give me radium, I must have cancer.' 'Oh,' I said, 'they treat everything now with radium. You would be in more pain if you had a cancer, and you wouldn't have lived this long.'

"That year Mr. Wolfe was operated on, I bought

Tom the last knickerbocker suit in Baltimore and shipped it on here. It was about the first of November and he wore that suit until Christmas when I bought him the suit with long pants. When I came home he said, 'What in the world did you buy some more short pants for?'

"That was the year Mr. Wolfe was operated on. He was operated on and took the radium treatment after that. He went to Johns Hopkins six or seven times. He walked across Broadway and going up in that main hospital there is a mammoth statue of Christ right in the lobby there, and it said, 'Come unto me all ye that labor,' and Mr. Wolfe said, 'If you've got the money.'

"Well, Mr. Wolfe was operated on at that time, and three years later he commenced suffering about as bad. I was in Chicago when he wrote to me about it, but he didn't go to Hopkins until the next February. Tom was at Chapel Hill when he went back for treatment. Mr. Wolfe was nervous and afraid about the operation, and we thought he was going to kill himself drinking. He had gone down to Mabel's and she brought him up here one Sunday afternoon, and he sobered up. He straightened up. They put him there in the hospital and treated him for about a week because Dr. Young wasn't ready to operate. I said, 'Do you think there's any danger in operating on Mr. Wolfe?' 'Oh,' said the doctor, 'he's the best preserved man I believe I have ever had—nothing wrong with any organ of his body.

He's in fine shape.' I looked at him and said, 'What are you talking about? I started ten days ago to come up here, and I thought he was going to drink himself to death. Why, he's a habitual drinker and I thought a man that drank so much couldn't stand the anaesthetic.' And he said, 'You mean to say he drinks?' They couldn't tell that—so little they know.

"While we were at the hospital another doctor told us, 'Dr. Hugh Young is operating on Wilson for the same trouble as Mr. Wolfe's.' And Mr. Wolfe said, 'I'll forgive all the bitterness I have had against Wilson.' He had criticized Wilson so bitterly, and then forgave him.

"Way back there Mr. Wolfe said, 'You went to see that Wilson inaugurated—a man that promised to keep us out of war.' I took Tom—he was twelve years old then—to Wilson's inauguration. We were on B Street and Wilson and Taft were riding up in the car, and had to make that turn and halted right in front of us. Some of the people hollered, 'Hurrah for Taft!' and some of them, 'Hurrah for Wilson!' and they would bow and smile, bow and smile.

"I was a Democrat; Mr. Wolfe was a Republican. As I say, he didn't care for Wilson at all. He would always vote the national ticket Republican . . . Well, I was standing right by a little tree with earth around it, and Tom right at my feet. I said to Tom, 'You go sit on the curb.' I had to stand, but I didn't get tired. Mr. Wolfe said, 'Keep that child out there all day long!' Tom had some lunch in a bag, bananas and things, but Mr. Wolfe said, 'Standing out there to see that old Wilson inaugurated!'

"But he changed. Wilson was operated on the next Saturday after he was, and he found out about it and said, 'Well, poor man, I have condemned him for a great many things and he was suffering and really wasn't guilty.' Mr. Wolfe took back most of the things he'd said about him."

I sat on the front porch with Mrs. Wolfe in the rocking chairs. A handsome automobile rolled slowly down Spruce Street and the occupants looked at us curiously.

"They've read Tom's books," his mother said. "They'll drive around town and then drive past here again. Maybe they'll stop in. Often I see people drive past and after a while drive past again. They look and look."

Later in the afternoon she expressed a desire to pay a visit to the cemetery. We went there and I noted a new grave on which young grass sprouted sparsely, in the Westall plot. She told me Elmer had passed on. She described his last illness in some detail.

"It's too bad," she said, "that they never did get to publish the pictures in *Life* while he was living. He used to look in the magazine every week, and he'd say, 'Julia, the pictures aren't in this week, they ought to have them in for sure next week.'"

Chapter Four

My third day at the Old Kentucky Home the weather went cold and the wind blew. The old house was tomb-chill. I sat with Mrs. Wolfe in the sun-parlor, but no sun shone. Mrs. Wolfe occupied herself with sewing in her lap. She appeared completely comfortable.

"Tom built all that about Greely," she said. "Greely was a brother of mine, between Crockett and Elmer, and when he was about five years old he became diseased in the way that his feet were dropsical; they commenced to swell and puff, and old Dr. Nelson said —oh, I don't know—gave him medicine and tried to keep him off his feet. He would put his finger down there and hold it a little, and it would leave a hole— but he didn't suffer. Old Dr. Nelson told Father, 'He will never live to manhood.' So they just let him do as he pleased, you know.

"He was kind of unbalanced. The teacher said, 'He knows more history than all the children in school.' But he couldn't learn the multiplication table. He didn't know a dollar from a five-dollar bill. But over at the old Asheville Female College, if they wanted to engage a musician to play they would call Greely in to listen to him first, and if Greely said he was all right, then they would hire him. They got a man here, and Greely said, 'Oh, I wouldn't get him—he's no musician.' Yet they employed him at Biltmore anyway, and had to dismiss him.

"He liked to hear Mr. Wolfe read poetry. And the disease—that was a prenatal effect. Mother used to cry when they would criticize Greely, said it wasn't Greely's fault. Well, he was a healthy-looking child up until he was five years old. He and Elmer used to have slates, and they would go up town and see a building and go home and draw it on their slates."

My feet were cold and I shifted them. "How many children were there?" I asked.

"Eleven. I was the fourth. I had a sister and two brothers older—Henry, Sam and Sally. Then I came in, then Jim, Will and Lee, and Mary between. Lee died something over a month before I was married. He was a fine looking boy. Then there were Crockett, Greely and Elmer.

"Crockett and Elmer were the great students. Elmer was a regular prodigy in mathematics. Greely was robbed of it. His teacher said she just didn't bother him any more about it. Tom has heard us talk about him. Tom never knew him. It is mostly fiction about Greely in Tom's book. He just knows enough to make a story out of it. I wrote Tom after 'Look Homeward,

Angel' came out, and I said, 'There are some things in there that remind you of facts.' I said there were things in it I would like to forget—little things . . . Sad things."

She lapsed into silence over her sewing. I picked up the copy of 'From Death to Morning' which she had brought out to show me. On the fly leaf in Thomas Wolfe's handwriting was an inscription to his mother, stating that the story, 'Web of Earth,' was her story.

She began again, after threading her needle:

"My brother Crockett and Uncle Bacchus were very congenial. Uncle Bacchus was the youngest of the first family. My grandfather was married twice, and Uncle Bacchus was the baby of the first family.

"I think there were six of them. One lost his life in the Civil War—Uncle William. I was too young to know him well, but they all said he was a brave soldier. They went out at the first call—Mother had two brothers and Father had two, and they went at first, and I never knew any of them until after the War when they came home. Uncle Jim, Mother's brother, and Uncle William were both killed—Uncle Jim in the Battle of Mannassas, and the next year, Uncle William, and I don't know just where, but his body was buried in Richmond, Virginia.

"Well, Uncle Bacchus at that time after he came back from the Civil War, he wasn't preaching. He didn't do that for some time after the Civil War. Say, he lived eighty-four years, and if he ever committed a sin, nobody knew it. He said that he was going to try to live on until Christ set up his kingdom—he wanted to be living at that time. Tom sat out there on the porch, taking it all in, not quite fourteen, and said, 'About what time do you think the beginning of this new era will take place?' And Uncle Bacchus said, 'Well, the way we figure it—we may have made some mistakes— but our figuring is about September of this year.'

"That was in 1914. And you know that war commenced over in Europe that same year. Uncle Bacchus went back, you know, back out West, and wrote to brother Crockett, says, 'I told you,' says, 'It's coming —it's coming.' The war, you know, the Battle of Armageddon.

"Uncle Bacchus preached and tried to live the perfect life. That was Uncle Bacchus . . .

"Say, the time when he was here . . ." She placed a finger against her nose and simpered. "I remember I had the house almost filled up and he wanted to stay here—now, I'll tell you:

"Uncle Bacchus seemed to be a very healthy man all his life, and he stayed at our house when I was a child, and Mother used to say that she tried to keep him supplied with clean hose or socks when he came in because she said his feet smelled so bad she couldn't stand him in the house.

"She always said, 'Here's a clean pair of socks. Now, go bathe your feet.' And I hadn't forgotten that when he came here. I told him, 'Uncle Bacchus, I'll put you right next the bathroom, and you'll probably want to wash your feet every night because after tramping around and around you'll feel so much better.'

"And I said, 'There is a chair—sit in the chair and put your feet over in the bathtub. There's plenty of water and all.'

"And he says, 'All right.' He went in the room—he would retire early. He went in the room and pulled off his shoes and went barefooted on his way to the bathroom. He came into the hall—nobody to see him—right over the carpet, and went into the bathroom and bathed his feet.

"Well, I went out in the hall after a while, and you know I couldn't stand the odor in that hall. I had to scrub that hall, I used lysol to destroy the odor. The next day I said, 'Uncle Bacchus, when you sat on that chair, didn't you pull off your shoes?' He said, 'I left them in the room,' and by then I knew what he had done. He said, 'I never thought,' and I said, 'You left all that scent on the carpet—so tonight you take off your shoes and put your feet in the tub and after you get through, put your socks in and wash them out, too.' I don't know, I guess it was the perspiration. Tom wrote the story, and he got it all mixed up in this other story about what those soldiers said about his feet. But Uncle Bacchus—after that I didn't smell any odor on the floor. But he was a good man."

The chill was depressing, and after excusing myself I

left the sun-parlor, imagining that by taking a brisk walk I might warm up a little. Outdoors a cutting wind blew, and I hadn't brought an overcoat to Asheville with me. I turned back into the hall, heavy in shadows this overcast day.

An icy trickle of water came from the faucet in the bathroom. For a few minutes I paced around upstairs in the cavernous hall, pausing now and then to peer into one of the silent chambers. The calcimined walls had a dour bluish hue. The chairs and wash-stands had an unearthly silence about them.

I returned to the sun-parlor, and Mrs. Wolfe looked up at me penetratingly for a moment. She went on with her sewing.

"Have you started writing anything about me?" she asked.

"Well, a few notes," I replied.

"When are you going to begin?"

"I haven't gathered enough material," I said.

"Well, write something that people will want to read," she said. "Paint it all up. One of these days I've got a mind to do it myself, and I'll write more on a page than you will, too. Say, I'll write something exciting and send it to the 'Ladies' Home Journal' or one of those magazines."

She sucked her thread to stiffen it for the needle's eye. "If I had the time, now—the leisure . . ."

Presently she was telling about her purchase of the Old Kentucky Home:

"Bought it from Rev. Meyers. T. M. Meyers. I saw him on the street before I bought this place, and he told me, 'I ought to be off on my lecture trip, but I haven't been well,' and I said, 'What is your trouble? You look well.' And he said, pointing to his head, 'There's something here gets crossed and I don't know my name or your name.'

"He drank. Maybe that was the matter. Claimed it was something wrong with his head. He would be perfectly normal, and then wouldn't know if he was T. M. Meyers or somebody else. He got up one morning about four o'clock or earlier, and Mrs. Meyers was in the same room and didn't see him go out. He went right out in his night clothes and walked all the way around the Square and down by the Baptist Church, and he went in the front room of a house there and crawled in bed. It was a Jewish woman that was living there, and she went in and found him and screamed and screamed. Then she saw who he was, and she sent over to Mrs. Meyers to get somebody to take him. But anyway, they claimed the trouble was with his head . . .

"I paid $7,000 for the house. But Mr. Meyers sold the alley as a joint alley, and the Sluders didn't use it any more. They lived over there, and this alley was supposed to go all the way through, but they had fenced it off, and he said, 'They will never use it, but it is a joint alley.'

"I planted shrubbery there and an old man that

rented the place came over here and said, 'Did you
know that alley doesn't belong to you?' And I said,
'I know all about that.' Mrs. Sluder came through one
day and I was planting some lilies, and she said, 'I will
sell you this alley,' and I said, 'I notice you don't use
it, it's fenced off.' And she said, 'I own seventeen feet,'
and I said, 'Mr. Meyers said it was a joint alley.'

"And she said, 'No, it is my alley—Mr. Sluder
bought this and gave it to his daughter and son-in-law,
but there was nothing said about the alley.' He may
have intended it as a joint alley, but that is where she
had us. She said, 'I'll sell it for $500.'

"I said, 'We certainly have to have the alley,' because we couldn't get into the rear on the other side.
So I told Mr. Wolfe and he was up in the air about it.
Said he would see her about it. I reasoned with him.
I said, 'We will have to have it. According to the contract it was a joint alley. We'll have to pay for one
half, no matter who owns the other half.'

"The lawyers commenced to search then, and they
found that there was nothing said about the alley in
the back deeds, and when the old man made his will
he left the old home place and that part that fronted
on Spruce Street, to his idiotic daughter, Maggie.

"Well, I said to Mr. Wolfe, 'Let's pay it off and be
done with it.' But he said, no, he was going to make
Meyers pay. I had paid $2,000 down and was to pay
$500 every six months, and there were two notes still

due. So he attached the balance of that until they settled it. Will Barnard had sold it to Jim Reynolds and his wife or Alice Reynolds, but they were all dead. But Mr. Carl Reynolds was administrator for his sister's estate, and Carl Reynolds and Will Barnard agreed to pay $250, if Mr. Meyers would pay the other $250. But I said, 'I'd just as well handed her the $500 the day she offered.' I said it would have been better to have paid instead of going to a lawyer. But Mr. Wolfe wanted to show them that they had to do something. Anyhow, it cost the $500 by the time they got through, the time, interest, and so forth, and we could have paid it off at the beginning. Arbitrate—don't go to a lawyer. And that's how it was—cost $7,500 in the end. But I got seventeen feet more of land added to it . . ."

I wriggled my toes coldly in my shoes. The chill undermined my confidence, but I said, "Mrs. Wolfe, do you remember in the first chapter of 'Of Time and the River,' they are waiting for the train, and Eliza Gant says to Eugene, 'You thought you were the youngest,' implying perhaps that there were other children who came after him—do you remember that, Mrs. Wolfe?"

She looked at me. Her expression was smiling, the smile half forced back, and she kept looking at me, but I could not see beyond the mask of her shining flat-looking brown eyes. Her head bobbed slightly, as if she had palsy, giving the impression that inner laughter caused her to shake slightly on the outside.

"Yes, I remember," she said.

"What did he mean when he wrote that?" I asked. "Were there supposed to have been others who came after?"

"Oh, he just wrote that to show every one's feelings were strained, waiting for the train to come," said Mrs. Wolfe. "They were talking about everything except what they were thinking about. They were on the point of parting, but they were talking about things to make talk."

She kept looking at me with pursed smile.

"What did Thomas call you?" I asked. "Mother or Mamma?"

"He called me Mamma always. But when he went down to Chapel Hill I found a few letters where he called me Mother. But when he was a boy and after he grew to be a man in New York or Boston or anywhere else, it was always Mamma. The children do to this day. Not one of them ever called me Mother. I suppose Mr. Wolfe told them to call me that. It was always Mamma."

"Was your family awfully poor after the Civil War?" I asked.

"Yes, everybody was poor. Everybody was poor in the South in this part of the country. This is a mountain country, not any farming country. All the darkies freed—nobody to do any work. Yes, we were poor . . . Will said we didn't meet, except at weddings and funerals. The reason was that we were so busy—none of us wanted to be poor. We didn't want our children to be poor like we were."

"What did Mr. Wolfe mean by 'mountain grill?'"

"I don't know where he got that," she replied. "I guess he made it up. A mountain grill must be somebody that is ignorant, not much above an animal. East Tennessee mountain grill. The East Tennessee people are entirely different from the western. Right up in these mountains here there were mountaineers with no education, not the slightest. If he wanted to make anybody mad he would say, 'Nothing but a mountain grill.'"

"Mr. Wolfe—how did he like being a stone-cutter?"

"He hated it. He would have liked being an actor. He'd go to Baltimore and Washington and see all the plays, Shakespeare and everything playing. He knew Washington like a checkerboard. Later on in life he would have liked to have been a lawyer, but when he was a boy it was an actor. But poverty cuts off lots of us from being what we would like.

"He said he didn't know why his mother put him to the trade of stone-cutter. Why back there you had to learn a trade—had to be an apprentice. That was the way it was in the stone business. They served as apprentices."

"Was it true," I asked, "that Mr. Wolfe as a young man could drink more liquor than any four average men?"

"I don't know how it was when he was a young man," she replied, "but after we married that was what they said he could drink. Dr. Purefoy would tell you how he drank. Lots of men that drink don't eat, but Mr. Wolfe would eat, and it was the food that kept the liquor from doing him so much harm. He was a spree drinker, and he would quit until he would take a spell again. But he would go through a brick wall to get it when one of those spells came on and he wanted it. The doctor said, 'Whiskey will kill a dram drinker quicker than it will kill Mr. Wolfe.'

"Mr. Wolfe became discouraged when he got sick and couldn't go ahead with his business. I knew he was sick, but we didn't let him know. I told him to let Cash Gudger come in with him, but he said oh no, there wasn't much business. I said, 'Well, remodel the building and rent it.'

" 'No, better sell it,' he said. I didn't want to sell it. He kept telling me, 'You keep me from selling it. The tax man will get it all.' I said, 'Well, improve the property and rent it.' No, he said it would take too much money.

"But I didn't want to sell that store building on the Square. One morning he said, 'I believe if I sell that building and get that off my mind, I'll get well. I've got an offer and Jess Law wants an option on it for thirty days.'

" 'Now,' I said, 'you don't want to sell it.' But he said, 'I believe I'll get well.' I said, 'Oh, Jess Law will never sell it. What did you tell him you would take for it?' He said $25,000 cash, net, too. He believed that he would get well after it was sold. Well, I had no idea that Jess Law would sell it. And I said, 'If it would make you happy, I'll sign the paper for you.'

"Well, it went on nearly three or four weeks. I kept worrying, wishing that thirty days would hurry and get out. I said to Mr. Wolfe, 'When does that option run out?' He said, 'Next Monday.' I said, 'I wish I could sleep till Monday. You don't want to sell it.' 'No,' he said, 'I don't think I do, but Jess Law has the option.'

"Well, he came home Saturday, and he looked pale, and he said, 'Jess Law has sold the building. What am I going to do?' 'Well,' I told him, 'you will have to let the sale go through or pay Jess Law his commission.' He worried—he had till Monday to make his decision. I said, 'Just let it go then, so long as he has sold it.'

"That same week they sold the home place. Dr. Purefoy was giving Mr. Wolfe some kind of medicine to quiet him, and he couldn't think like he ought to. Dr. Purefoy would give him that medicine and he took too much of it. I called up Dr. Purefoy one night and said, 'Mr. Wolfe has got to stop taking that medicine.' He said, 'Well, hide it.' 'Hide it nothing,' I said. 'He goes to the phone and calls up Aiken and Hester and gets another bottle whenever he wants to.' I was afraid Mr. Wolfe might fall out on the back porch or somewhere.

He said, 'I think he needs an attendant.' I said, 'I think he needs a doctor.'

"So I told Mr. Wolfe after he sold the old home place, 'Now, we are going to come back up here.' I had rented this place out and the woman owed me some rent, and I didn't see any chance of getting it. I said, 'Mr. Wolfe, you're coming up here and Dr. Purefoy isn't going to cross that threshold.' That's how Dr. Glenn got to waiting on Mr. Wolfe. I told Dr. Glenn, 'That old dope doctor! I just live in dread if Mr. Wolfe comes on that back porch after he has taken some of that medicine, and falls down those back steps.'

"I told him to go over to Aiken and Hester and see what was in the prescription. He went over there and looked at it and said it wasn't exactly a dope. He said, 'I can get him off it in two weeks,' and in two weeks time Dr. Glenn said to Mr. Wolfe, 'Things don't appear to you like they did, do they?' And Mr. Wolfe said he felt different.

"I was worried about selling the home place. Mr. Wolfe sold four pieces of property in one week's time, but he insisted it must be sold. Said he would get well then. It was the effect of that medicine."

I questioned Mrs. Wolfe regarding her own sicknesses, and she shuddered, saying, "It would be terrible to tell all that. I could go back to Shakespeare and say, 'I came into the world scarce half made up.' Mother said she worked too hard the year before I was born,

79

and when I came I was nothing but skin and bone. I was so homely she used to cover me up to keep people from seeing me. When I was a girl growing up people thought I was pretty good looking, and she used to tell them, 'When she was a little baby I used to cover her to keep people from knowing I had a baby.'

"She felt guilty, of course. I was sick all the time it seemed to me. I can remember nearly every week growing up I was hindered from going out to play. I guess that was why Father clung to me.

"But I must have had a constitution back of it all. I kept on going, lived on my will maybe. Had all the ailments that flesh has been heir to, and came through. When I taught school I weighed a hundred and nineteen pounds. I was out in the country—taught a country school first. When I went there I couldn't walk much. It was nearly two miles to the schoolhouse. I lived with the Baileys, and Wesley Bailey and I walked. At first, I could walk about half a mile and was worn out, but before I got through, in a year's time, I could beat any of the country people walking. That was what the country did for me. I could walk anywhere or do anything.

"Those people who lived in the country just worshipped me. I was the head of everything that happened there, and there was a sense of pride that you felt that —well, that you are somebody here, and you might go some place else and only be an atom there. At home they would write as if I was out of the world. Friends

Land Below the Wind. By Agnes
ewton Keith. Boston: Little, Brown.

Land Below the Wind is a somewhat
oetic title for autobiographical adven-
ires in Borneo, an island most fre-
iently heralded as the home of wild
en and head hunters. In addition to
e wind, Mrs. Keith should have in-
uded something about the rain, in
der to prepare readers for the deluges
at drench her pages. This is one in-
ance, however, when dampness is but
somber background for the gay spirit
an individual who grew hot with
pectation and cold with premonition,
d had the courage for any adventure.
The author's business in Borneo was
erely that of wife of the Conservator
Forests and Director of Agriculture
North Borneo, a position that re-
ired an abundance of diplomacy to
ep peace among five servants of dif-
ent nationalities. In addition to the
vants the household livestock in-
ded from three to a dozen semi-
mese cats, one dog, two gibbon apes,
netimes an orang-utan, and visiting
gle animals.

While Sandakan, six weeks by boat
m California, is not a place where
atives come to spend their vacations,
there were often interesting visitors
break the monotony, and Mrs. Keith
ites at length about Osa and Martin
nson's last expedition. The Keiths'
lidays were spent exploring the
nds in the Sulu Sea, and to do them
tice she says one needs "words that
cut and polished and set in precious
nes, Tiffany words of rare work-
nship used for flawless gems." But
every day was bright, for there were
ticks, mosquitoes, sand fleas, and of
rse rain. During one storm they had
wrap their house in a great bronze
to keep it together.

Mrs. Keith's writing has such in-
iduality, one is not surprised that
book was awarded the $5,000 At-
ic nonfiction prize.

E MAN'S WIFE

an you stay out there among
hey thought there was no so-
d to it and loved the people
d did any and everything for

ley fiddled at the big dances,
he quiltings, the only amuse-
the men would take a bottle
people thought anybody that
ng to hell. And I played the
my way through. I had some
't have a piano. It was only
ays and Cheeseboroughs that
d the violin when I was about
ought a violin or fiddle, and
e to see Father and Mother,
that violin and played. They
, 'We didn't know you could
the fiddle.' I played church
at's just what that fiddle was
sic, not dancing.'
widower—he was one of your
d glove men, what you call a
topped at our house to stay
stopped because I wanted to
for him, and he told Uncle
ght at the Westalls because I
play.' Uncle Bob came over

81

and said, 'It's all right to play for younger people, but to play for an old man and run him crazy, that's going to far.'

"I stopped playing when I got married. But sometimes the old feeling comes back . . . There was a man came here, Professor Chase from New York, he had a class of sight reading. Asheville was only a little country town then . . . Out there at Chimney Rock—it was called Bear Wallow—there was a family named Freeman. They were all good musicians, had good voices, all could sing. Alec Porter was a friend of mine, about twelve years older, but an old bachelor. He had a store there and we lived nearby. When I was a child he was grown. Mr. Porter was a hunter and had a great big bear skin, and they would wrap themselves up in that and try to scare us. It would scare Jim. And Alec and Bob would run around the house trying to kiss me . . . But when I grew up they didn't have to chase me."

She smiled over her thoughts, her lips trembling and twitching.

"We went to the sight reading class," she continued. "Lula Reed was with us. She was in love with Alec, but she was too young for him. She would tease him and say, 'You and Julia are going to get married some day.' And he would say, 'Oh no, she's too high strung.' We started up the Swannanoa one night on a sleigh, but it got to melting and we had to come back.

"There were bears around there when I was a girl,

and wolves too. They were the old black bears. Uncle
William went up on the Seven Mile Ridge over in
Yancey County to put a bear trap up there, and of
course, he had to go up to see if he had caught a bear.
One day he went up there and came back and said he
got out on a flat rock and saw a rattlesnake. He had his
gun and killed the snake. The rock commenced to move
and then the snakes commenced to crawl out. That
must have been the old snake—and there were seven
others. He killed them all and came back one day as
unconcerned, and he said, 'You'll have to bring a mule
and some of you come to help. Largest bear I ever saw
—seven hundred pounds, I think.' They had to take a
mule and a rope and drag it down the mountain. There
were no roads up there, just a path. You don't find such
bears nowadays, though they say there are some in the
Pisgah Forest now.

"Those days I could have shot down a wild turkey
most any time. Henry killed a ground hog and they
brought it home and skinned it and mother baked that
ground hog. There is no young chicken I ever tasted
that was better.

"And say, I had the prettiest one down in this back
lot. There used to be an old stable down there, and I
don't know how it got here unless somebody brought it
to town and it escaped. But it was the prettiest ground
hog, reddish brown, and it used to come down in the
fall of the year and go down there in the garden, and
there was a little young peach tree. They hold their

leaves longer in the fall of the year. I watched that ground hog and I said, 'It's going to try to eat those green leaves.' The bush was too small to hold his weight. Finally he reached up with his paw and pulled the limb down and held it between his feet and ate the leaves off that branch. A negro came across there one day and said, 'Is that your ground hog?' And I said, 'Yes, everything here is mine. That is my pet.'"

I rose. "Mrs. Wolfe, I guess I'll go out to supper."

She cocked an eye up at me. "All right," she said cheerfully. "You run along, then."

I left the house and hurried up the slope of Spruce Street to the Square. The restaurant was warm.

Chapter Five

That night the wind howled around the Old Kentucky Home. I sat with Mrs. Wolfe in the parlor before a coke blaze in the open fireplace.

"Falling in love is out of fashion," she was saying. "The times and the people have changed, that is all. There was a time that I can remember when I was a girl, if anybody got divorced, they were looked upon as criminal and you just steered clear of them. I remember once at church away up at Swannanoa, the Whites were there with a very good looking woman, and I asked Mother who was that, and she said, 'Don't even mention her—she is a divorced woman.' And I thought she was a good looking woman. 'Don't say a word,' Mother said, 'she is a divorced woman.'

"When people were married they stuck. Took them for better or worse, and if it was worse, just stuck to their bargain. Like I stuck to Mr. Wolfe. I remember one day, I only had two children—that was Frank and Effie—I don't know what it was Mr. Wolfe and I had been discussing, but I was dusting and Mr. Wolfe said, 'You are the hard, the most hard-hearted woman I ever knew.' It was about something, I don't know what it was. I looked around, and I said, 'I have been married to a marble man,'—that was what they called the kind of business he was in—'a marble man so long that I am petrified.' And I looked at him and he was laughing to himself about it."

The wind hurried around the corner of the house with a little whine.

"It was a night like this," she said, "the night before Selmar died . . . I'll tell you about that:

"He must have come to my house about 1924. I was already spending my winters in Miami, Florida. His birthplace was Sioux City, Iowa. He was in the World War, and he may have been gassed in France. I do not know why he came here unless he felt it was a good healthful place. His family never knew why he wanted to stay in Asheville. Stayed at my house about eleven years, and was here when 'Look Homeward, Angel' came out.

"I gave him my book to read. He said, 'They make a big fuss now, but one day they will recognize Tom as a great writer.' Tom knew him quite well. When Tom came home for a while and went away again, he said, 'Well Selmar, you take care of Mamma and let Mamma take care of you.' He said that in the car to go to the station.

"Selmar's drinking was his misfortune. He would say, 'I'm going to leave tomorrow, going to get a room tomorrow.' Then, 'I must stay until Monday, until my check comes.' He stayed there a whole winter, so I just got mad and went off to Florida. I knew he would do as he pleased anyway . . . It was 1933 or 1934, the year of the Fair, and he took cold while I was gone. He stayed up so late at night and would not get up until two or three o'clock in the afternoon. He read all night. But just before I left on the trip, he said, 'Get me a clock, I want to get up in the morning about seven o'clock. Joe McIntyre got in a load of fruit and I promised to go up there to help him.'

"I got him the clock. This was before I left. When I got back home he had a terrible cold, and I said I guess it is getting up too early in the morning and going out to help Joe. I noticed a slight fever coming out and he had a cough, had a good cough. I said, 'Now, he will get pneumonia if he doesn't get to bed.' I said, 'Stay there and I will feed you until you get over this cold.' I said, 'You should have had it broken up long ago.'

"I moved him over to Mr. Doddy's room that had a stove in it. It was in the fall of the year, November first. He asked what his temperature was and I said one hundred degrees. I wanted to get it down. I said, 'Now you stay in bed until Monday or it will be two hundred by Monday morning,' and he said, 'You're the doctor and I must obey.' That was Friday and he seemed all right.

"Saturday night I went to the store to buy some things. When I got back Selmar was sitting there by

himself by the stove in the hall. I said, 'Who told you
to get up?' He said he came down to use the phone
and work a crossword puzzle. He said, 'I will go right
back.'

"Well, I went back to put the groceries away, then
came back to see if he needed anything. I said, 'Don't
misplace my paper,' and he said, 'I will put it back
where I got it.'

"Well, he went on upstairs and I did not see him any
more. I heard him coughing. I knew he had throat
trouble—had burned his throat earlier by drinking
Red Devil lye—he said they sold it to him for whiskey.

"Sunday morning about ten o'clock I had taken a cup
of tea and had poured out his to give it to him. I
reached around to pick up one of those little skull caps
to put on—when I heard a noise. I looked at the stove
and there he stood, at the swinging door. His mouth
was just pouring blood—he held his hand over it to
keep it from spilling on the floor. He said, 'Call a doctor.' I said, 'Lie down.' His head went near the bathroom door and I had hardly room to pass through to
the dining-room door. I looked out the window and saw
Mr. Dunn, the undertaker, across the street coming
out on his way to church. I told him to come quick. He
came and I said get his blankets off his bed to cover
him. He told me there was no need to get them. Two
boys from the house in back came over. The coroner
came. They just stood there and looked at him. I picked
up a sheet from the ironing board in the kitchen and

put it over him. He had his pajama suit on and stockings. No slippers. I just had a big coat on, and I went back to get some clothes on. The undertaker carried him across the street. They took him out while I was dressing.

"After he died I found in his room Mabel's address in Washington, tacked behind the dresser on the wall. He pasted it behind the dresser so he would have it handy in case he wanted it. He was to wire her if anything happened to me. He never told me about it, and I found it when I went to clean the room. He wasn't demonstrative at all, but when I used to come home from a trip he would go to some of the neighbors and say, 'The old lady is back—we have more fun; she can make more fun than any sixteen-year-old girl.' But he would never make any fuss over me. Tom said, 'Don't turn him out—he thinks the world of you.' "

I bent closer to the coke fire. My back and shoulders felt cold.

"But that coughing," Mrs. Wolfe said, looking into the fire and shaking her head with an expression of repugnance. "It made me think of Sally . . .

"Sally had never had a day of sickness except whooping cough and measles. I was the sickly one. It was the week that Tilden and Hayes were voted on, but they cheated Tilden out of it and Hayes was elected. If I had been Hayes, I wouldn't have accepted it.

"That was the week she took cold. I look back over

it now and wonder why Father and Mother didn't do something to break up that cold. One day—she had had the cold five or six weeks—and I remember she was on the back steps crying, and I said, 'It's because you cough so loud.' She said, 'No, I've got consumption. I spit up part of my lungs.' Then she said to come and she would show me. And we went, and there was an old flat rock, and on it what looked like the lungs of a chicken. I said, 'You just tore a little something loose—it will get all right.'

"She coughed on. There was no doctor called in. She took what we would call neuralgia in her jaws, and it commenced to swell. This was November, and she died the eighteenth of next April. She commenced to swell, and had to drink milk through a quill. Finally the cough stopped, and these glands began to swell. The only doctor that was over was Dr. Hilliard.

"She had a knot that was soft, up on top of her head. They called the doctor in as he was passing. Father and Mother went in the large room across the hall where she stayed. Father came out first after the doctor left, and came in and sat down at the dining table, and I said, 'What did Dr. Hilliard say caused those lumps to swell there?' Father didn't answer—he gave a quick jerk of the head. He said, 'He thinks it's scrofula.' I said, 'Scrofula—what's that?'

"There was a man came back from the Civil War, and he had a place on his knee, but still he was able to tend his farm. I said, 'Will she be an invalid? What causes it?' He said, 'I don't know. It might be inherited back from the seventh generation. If it didn't come out before the fourth it will skip until the seventh, that's what the doctor says.'

"Then Jim and I went to reading . . . It was nothing in the world but that cold, and when the cough stopped that poison was in the blood stream. She would say, 'Why, here's another one of those places.' The doctor left a little lancet to lance those places. She didn't seem to suffer, and I thought she would be an invalid—that she would live like Mr. Davidson to be old, but an invalid. I never thought of death."

Mrs. Wolfe took the poker and stirred the fire.

"One night I dreamed that Sally and I were both dead and lying on a trundle bed in front of that front window, and Mother and all the people were gathered around, and I said to Sally, 'What are they crying about our old dead bodies for? We are sitting here, and why don't they look at us? Come on and let's go round and make Mother understand we are still here.' She said, 'We're spirits.' And I said, 'We look just like we always did. I don't see why they don't know where we are.' And we went around to Mother, and I pulled and pulled at her sleeve, but she didn't pay any attention. It worried me, and I turned round and said, 'I can't make them see us.'

"And I looked then, and she was in the bed, but I wasn't, I was with the crowd. The scene changed, and she was laid out with a sheet right in front of those windows. The bed was gone. And later on I opened that kitchen door, where you could look across to the chimney back there. The rain was coming down in great big drops and that bed, just the stead, was leaning up against that chimney and the rain was pouring down on it. I said, 'Oh, oh, that horrible sight!' and I woke.

"I told Mother about it next day, but I had no thought of Sally dying. It was a month or so before she died. Three days before she died she took shortness of breath, and Mother came in where I was and said, 'She won't be here much longer.' Mrs. Cheeseborough and one of the girls came down. Sally was in the old high-posted bed and it didn't have any casters, but was against the wall. Mother and Father slept in the other bed in the same room, and she sat up all the time up till this time. Mrs. Cheeseborough remarked to Father, 'If you had an old-fashioned trundle bed to put here in the middle of the floor, you could walk all around and wait on her so much better.'

"Father said, 'I have some lumber and I can soon make one.' And then Sunday night came, and I remember I went in and had a cup of lemonade in my hand. They had been using lemonade to moisten her lips. She hadn't spoken above a whisper since Monday. I gave her some lemonade and she whispered, 'That's enough.' I sat it down, and my grandmother and my cousin were there and had just thrown themselves across the bed. Addie said to me, 'Come here and sit down.' Father and Mr. Brevard were near the fireplace, and Mother was lying on her bed. Everything was so quiet you could hear a pin drop.

"I sat down on the bed and threw myself back. And Sally said in a loud voice, 'Well, I'm going to die.' She hadn't spoken above a very low whisper since Monday, and only in monosyllables. Everybody jumped. Father came over and took one of the pillows from under her head. But she was gone.

"We went out of the room, and Mr. Brevard went for some of the neighbors, the Reeds and Creasmans lived quite a little distance. We went into the dining room, a great big old room. There was a bed over in one corner. We were in there and along about three or four o'clock Addie said, 'Let's go in the kitchen and make a pot of coffee.' We went into the kitchen and she started to make the coffee, and I opened the kitchen door, and it was raining, and there was that bed up against the chimney.

"I screamed, 'Oh, where have I seen that bed before! Where? Where?' I said, 'Oh, I have seen that bed there before—I have seen her lying out in front of that window on that bed!'

"Mother came to the kitchen and Addie said, 'Julia's lost her mind,' and Mother came up and put her arm around me. But how did I see that new bed when we didn't have it, and no one had said anything about it? Why, it was weeks before when I had the dream—and the rain was pouring down just as I had seen it in the dream. It has always been a mystery to me . . . If we had had a trundle bed—but we hadn't. Father had just made it, just finished it, and I had never seen it. Why was it that the dream came to me before that? I said, 'Oh, I have seen it,' and the rain was pouring down on it, and the light shone out of the kitchen right onto that bed."

She looked at me keenly, as if to see what I thought and when I said nothing, she shook her head, sucking in her lips. On the wall I caught sight of the stone-cutter's picture. I thought he looked inhospitable.

"She died the eighteenth of April in her nineteenth year," Mrs. Wolfe continued. "She was two years and six months older than I. She was born the eleventh day of September, and would have been twenty years old the next September. We buried her at the Newton Academy, and they moved all those graves quite a long while afterward. They wanted the remains all there so they could put the markers all together.

"Well, five weeks after she died, Grandmother was visiting us again. Now you may call this a dream, but I think it was a vision. Sally and Grandfather came in the door and Father looked at me and said, 'Don't ask any questions now. This is their first visit and they aren't strong enough.'

"At that time I never disobeyed my father, but I didn't know whether they would ever come again, and I didn't want to miss a chance. She sat down beside me, and Father wasn't looking at me, and I spoke to her in a very low voice. We went to the door, and there weren't any such things as searchlights then, but it was like a mammoth searchlight going into space, and we flashed over that into a new world. I saw the most beautiful flowers and birds. I said, 'Oh, they're wonderful.' 'Yes, but come on,' she said, 'we haven't time, we must hurry.' I looked ahead and there came a man on a white horse. I said, 'Oh, horses here, too!' The man stopped and put his hand out and patted me on my head, and I said, 'Anybody would fall in love with that man.' And she said, 'Come on.' I asked her about different people. She said, 'They're all here, but we haven't time.'

"I said, 'I don't want to go back.' But she said, 'It isn't your time. You must go back.' I said, 'Oh, where's Sam?' And she said, 'He's in a higher, happier sphere.' I said, 'Aren't you happy?' And she said, 'As happy as I know how—but we come here prepared to be happier later on.' She said, 'Now you must go back and wait your time.' We went over that white way in a flash. We stood and said goodbye, and she and Grandfather left.

"I looked at my father and said, 'Oh, they are gone,' and I was lying in the bed all aquiver. Father looked at me sternly and said, 'I told you to be quiet.' Afterwards I asked him why he said that to me, and he said he didn't know, the words just came. I studied about it all the next day. My grandmother was visiting, and she said, 'Julia, you act today as if you weren't here.' And I said, 'I haven't been here—I've been traveling everywhere.'

"The poor old woman thought I had lost my mind. I said, 'I have been with my sister in heaven.' She looked wildly at me, and I said, 'You might call it a dream, but it was a reality.' She said, 'Sit down and tell me all about it.' I said, 'Grandmother, I wanted to stay there.' And she said, 'Oh lord, if I was to have such an experience, I would go crazy. Didn't Sally tell you to come back and wait your time? I lost three of my family in a year and eight months—they all went when their time came,' my grandmother said.

"After that I suppose she must have told it when she went back to Swannanoa, because when Alec Porter went on a visit there, he came back and said, 'Don't ever tell another of your dreams.' He said the people grabbed at him and wanted to know had he heard about Julia Westall's dream . . .

"Well, Sally was dead—but I saw my father *when he was still living.*"

She looked at me with great intensity.

"I mean," she said, "that I saw a vision of him. He was building a home for John Patton. That was after the Civil War, and there were a lot of mean negroes. We would stand out and wait for him, and Mother would take up supper when she saw him coming. Well, he had said that morning that Mrs. Patton said she would gather some apples and he would bring some home that night.

"We were out on the porch waiting for Father, and it was a little later than he usually came, and I saw him coming just beyond the fence bars. He had a white bag over his shoulder, and I said, 'Oh, he's got the apples.' He came on up, and I said, 'Oh, where has he gone? He's disappeared.' Mother had gone to take up supper, and I said, 'Oh, he's disappeared.'

"But there wasn't anywhere for him to go. Henry was sitting over in the corner with his slate and didn't like to give up anything he was doing. Mother said, 'Henry, come here.' He got up, and I showed them just where Father came to, but he wasn't there. The others went to bed, but Sally and I stayed up with Mother. She thought that going through the woodland somebody might have murdered him, or he fell off the house. We were sitting there and it might have been eight or nine o'clock when we heard footsteps in the yard and knew there was more than one walking. Mother commenced to rub her hands, 'Oh, they've come to tell us about the news.'

"Uncle Bob Patton opened the door, and Father was right behind him. He had the apples in a pillow slip, and I said, 'Where did you go? I saw you.' Uncle Bob said, 'Blame me for it, I'm the one who is to blame for keeping him.' I jumped up on my father's lap and told him what I saw, said, 'You crossed the bars down there and you came up halfway, and disappeared.' He said,

'I guess it was my spirit came over here, because I thought about coming over, but they persuaded me to stay till after supper.' "

She struck at a chunk of coke until the sparks flew.

"Say, talking of seeing a person who isn't there—his other self—Tom has a story about Uncle Bacchus, but it was Father that was in it. Tom has it all twisted around . . . Father was brought up right when he was a child. His mother was a good woman, a good Presbyterian, and Sunday morning they all had to go to Sunday school.

"Well, after so long a time she went back to that big old kitchen—my grandfather was a hatter, and over in the corner was a big wool box. He made good hats, too. He must have been a good hatter. I saw a man twenty years or more after he died, and he said, 'I'll go down and see Sam'—Uncle Sam followed the same trade—and this old man said, 'I bought this hat twenty years ago—it's one of old Billy Westall's hats, when he made them they lasted.'

"Anyway, she went in there and saw Father lying asleep in the wool box. 'Well,' she said, 'I never knew him to do anything like that before.' But she thought she would let him sleep, and when she went back he wasn't in there. She thought, 'That's a trick—he wanted to miss Sunday school.'

"Then they all came home together, and she said, 'Why did you get in the wool box and go to sleep? I saw you in there.' And he said he hadn't been in the wool box. The older girl—Caroline—was a very bright girl with all the principle that belongs to a first-class woman, but Grandfather had brought her home from South Carolina from the market there when he traveled to sell his hats and bring back goods. He traveled in a four-horse wagon, once or twice a year. Well, he brought that girl home—she was several years older than any of Grandmother's children—and said, 'Children, here's your sister. She has come home to live.' He never explained to anybody about that girl. I don't suppose he did to his wife, and nobody ever asked Grandfather about it, though he didn't have a child at home that looked as much like him.

"Well, she was a girl of principle and her word could be relied on, and she said Father had been with them in Sunday school all the time."

Mrs. Wolfe was silent. The coke crackled slightly. The wind buffeted the house in thrusts. The cold stood at my shoulder, though face and hands were warm from the fire.

"Now that's mighty queer, isn't it?" she said. "But let me tell you something. It's about Tom's great-grandfather. First, I will say that I didn't know him way back there. He wasn't an educated man, but they said he had ideas that the astronomers brought out twenty years later. He lived over in Yancey County, and his oldest son, Uncle Sam, lived right near where I taught school. Uncle Sam, he is the one that we called the lazy one of the family. He talked religion all the time, argued religion. Well, he went up there to visit—it was about twelve miles, and Grandfather says, 'I'm awful glad you came. I have lots to talk about. I'm going to die tomorrow at ten minutes to six.'

"Uncle Sam says, 'Why, you aren't sick are you?' And Grandfather said, 'No, just usual health.' I don't know that he ever had any great sickness. Anyway, they talked and talked. Uncle Sam argued religion. He believed in the second coming of Christ. They talked the balance of the day, and they went to bed that night and slept in the same room. Uncle Sam liked to go to bed and lie there and talk, but he didn't sleep. They talked until late, and the next morning Uncle Sam hadn't forgotten, and said, 'If I were you, I'd just stay in bed—you'll feel better. I had just as soon stay in bed, too.'

"Well, they talked until almost six o'clock, and the time came, and he turned over in the bed with his face to the wall and died. Yet there wasn't anything the matter with him. Maybe he had had some liver or kidney trouble, but he either made up his mind or had some kind of premonition."

"Didn't Thomas have some sort of premonition, too?" I asked.

"Yes—but I'm going to tell you: Father took sick. I believe it was ptomaine poisoning. He got very sick and I asked him what could have made him so sick, and he didn't know unless it was some fish he ate. He went out to brother Jim's on Chestnut Street and was out there nearly two weeks. We went there every few days, and on Thursday I took Tom with me. Tom was named for him and he seemed to think more of him. On Friday I didn't take Tom—Tom wasn't feeling very well—and Captain Farrow was waiting on Father.

"He was dozing off, and opened his eyes. 'Hello Julia, how's Tom?' 'I didn't bring him,' I said. 'I'll wait until next time,' I said. He closed his eyes, and in a few minutes he said—and it wasn't twelve o'clock yet—'Is it six o'clock?' I said, 'No, you better sleep.' He dozed off again and then said, 'Is it six o'clock yet?' and Captain Farrow said, 'No, it isn't six o'clock yet.'

"I said, 'What does that mean—six o'clock?' He said, 'He's asked it several times.' Yet he was sensible about everything else. Well, I didn't stay so long because he looked like he was sleeping. Saturday afternoon he commenced to suffer terribly. He said, 'Well, if I don't get better, you'll have to take me to the cemetery.' He didn't say 'cemetery,' he said 'Newton Academy.' I think peritonitis had set in. He commenced to swell right up. Sunday morning they called up and said he had been sick all night. I don't think he talked any that day at all. He had gotten too low in the bed, and Mr. Wolfe said, 'We are going to put him further up in the bed—he'll be more comfortable.'

"And Mr. Wolfe and the others lifted him, Mr. Wolfe saying, 'Major, are you comfortable?' He said 'Yeh.' It was a bright Sunday afternoon. There was a clock on the mantle, and Dr. Purefoy was there, and several people standing around. The last breath went out just as the clock stopped striking six. I said, 'He asked if it was six o'clock and went out with the clock.' They said it was exact with Washington time, that clock."

"Do you think the Westalls had the power of foreseeing?" I asked.

She plucked thoughtfully at her lips. "Yes, they're kind of psychic. Father used to come in and say his dual self was walking beside him . . . I'm that way, too. It's usually, though, when my health's run down a little. I've got a little book that tells the reason people can't communicate with the spiritual world—says they eat too much meat, they belong to the earthy.

"Say, did you ever go into a room and feel somebody else there beside you? I have many a time. Sometimes I have heard Fred and Mabel calling me. They weren't in town. I would be upstairs there. I remember one day I said, 'All right, Mabel, I'll be down in a minute.' 'Hello, Mamma, Mamma.' And I came down and there wasn't anybody down there . . . Listen, and I'll tell you something."

The tremble in her low husky voice sent a chill up the roots of my hair, and glancing back I saw the portraits of the mature Thomas Wolfe and the pre-adolescent Thomas Wolfe in curls regarding me earnestly.

"It was back there in the Nineties when we used to read so much together," she said. "When I was busy sewing or something, he would read, and maybe he would want to smoke, and he would hand it over to me. We read 'When Knighthood Was in Flower' and a lot of others.

"But there was a book—I don't know what this book was now. He had been reading the book—I was busy. So many children, sewing and all, and he had been reading the book, and it got to be nine o'clock, and he wanted to smoke. He said, 'Say, there aren't many more chapters now—you finish the book.' I laid my work down and I read and finished the book. It was October twenty-six, and all the summer—I'll go back now— most of the summer I had had something wrong with my liver. I had a hard cough. I knew it wasn't from my lungs, but it was from my liver. I have been told that a pressure against the liver causes a cough like a tubercular cough.

"Well, this night, the twenty-sixth, when I finished the book, I went across the room to get some water. Mr. Wolfe always kept the room so warm. I came back in the room and went back to the fire, and took a chill. I went over there and lay down on the lounge and commenced to chill worse. I said, 'Well, I better go to bed.' It was nearly eleven o'clock. I got upstairs and had another hard chill. I got the colored girl who slept in the back room, I said, 'You heat the water. I'm going to take a warm bath and get warm.'

"Now, we'll go back. Through the summer I couldn't lie down—I had about seven pillows piled around me.

I slept in the room with the children—three beds in that room. I had a little tiny lamp that was over on a washstand, and on the other side of the wall was Mr. Wolfe's room. After I went to bed I said, 'Oh, this cough!' I had a pain in my liver and all. I said, 'I don't believe I'll ever get through this summer.' I had told him time and again, 'I don't believe I'll ever get through.'

"Just imagine somebody putting their arm around your shoulders. I hadn't been in bed five minutes, thinking how long could I go on. They put their arm around me and sort of squeezed me and whispered in this ear, 'Two—two,' and over at that window another voice called out loud, 'Twenty-twenty.'

" 'So I'm going to die in two weeks or twenty days,' I said. 'That's what it means.'

"Mr. Wolfe said, 'You were dreaming.' I said, 'I haven't been in bed long enough to dream. I was lying here looking at that little light over there.' He said, 'Oh, you're going to be all right.'

"You know, I never thought anything more about that. I got along. I was telling you about the twenty-sixth. Grover and Ben were born on the next day, the twenty-seventh. Mr. Wolfe went after the doctor, and I said, 'Doctor, I don't know why they have sent for you—it's two weeks yet before you ought to come.' He said, 'It's your time.' Mr. Wolfe went up town that day. On the street he met the editor of the paper and Mr.

Wolfe said to him, 'Benjamin Harrison and Grover Cleveland have come to my house and they have come to stay.' It was the twenty-seventh of October and the first Tuesday in November was election.

"Mr. Wolfe came home, and, I believe it was that night or the next day, he said, 'Here you are—you're all right and you've got two babies—I counted it up, and it has been just exactly twenty days since you called me into the room, and here it all figures out.' And I said, 'You're right about that.' He said, 'People get worried about things. It didn't mean that you were going to die at all.' That is the background for 'The Web of Earth.' That's what Tom made use of. Those spirits didn't say I was going to die—they encouraged me and squeezed me and said, 'Two—two,' and the other said, 'Twenty-twenty.' "

"Was the story of the murderers in 'Web of Earth' based on facts?" I asked.

"Oh, that was Ed Ray and Waites Anderson," she replied. "Tom calls them Ed Mears and Laurence Wayne."

"Did the escaped murderer really come to your house?"

"No, he didn't come here. Up to that time Tom told about facts. But that was fiction about the murderer coming here. I knew him, though, and the only good thing I found in that story was that Ed Ray or Ed Mears came and said he came because he could trust me—came to get a pair of shoes. That is the fiction that I went to the closet and gave him a practically new pair of shoes."

The fire was burning low. She raked the embers. She said, "The difference between me and Mr. Wolfe, he said I burned more coal than he did, but I never had a warm fire."

I went upstairs. The coldness was so bitter as to seem to exert pressure. I went to bed immediately and shivered in the icy sheets. There were many blankets over me, and shortly, my knees drawn up, I became warm. But I could not sleep. Outside the wind made noises, and within the house there were creakings, faint indeterminate snappings and sighs.

I wondered how many of the Wolfes had slept in the bed where I huddled. How many men now departed? Perhaps someone had died in this very bed. Certainly Ben and his father and the homeless Selmar had died within these walls. I felt their spirits abroad in the dank, dark rooms.

The great Thomas—his mother had said he couldn't find a bed in the house long enough for his length—I fancied his giant ghost returned home at last and in a silent rage because there was a stranger who had come to ply his old mother with questions. And Cynthia, the red-headed consumptive—I thought of her ghost manifesting itself as the smell of musty winter when I thrust my nose out of the covers a little. I heard secret whispers which were gone before I could focus my attention —slight sibilants impossible to account for, as if the ancient house were echoing ever so faintly the events of buried days. I felt a malignancy in the air. Ah, curse him, curdle his blood with mounting horror, this stranger with a typewriter who has come boldly and lies unprotected now in bed!

I threw off the blankets. I put on the light and looked around. The hairs on my arms and the back of my neck stood up. Soon I had dressed, and I went down the wide carpeted stairs in the dim light of a single low-powered electric bulb, with my bag and the portable.

I went to the Asheville-Biltmore hotel, got a room, took a bath, went to bed and slept immediately. The room was too expensive for my means, and the next morning I got a room at a Mrs. Moore's. She was a comfortable graying woman, and she had heat in the house. She said that she knew Mrs. Wolfe. I gathered that as competing landladies, there was no great love lost between the two.

I returned to the Old Kentucky Home that morning to let Mrs. Wolfe know I had made the change. I had supposed she would imagine I was still in bed, but I found her, looking grim, in the sun-parlor.

"Why didn't you tell me you were leaving?" she demanded, more fierce than I had thought she could be.

"I looked into your room before I went to bed last night, to see if you were all right, and you were gone."

"I'm sorry I didn't let you know," I mumbled. "I should have let you know—well, I decided it wasn't fair to accept your kindness to me—and expect you to wait on me—make my bed and everything . . ."

"I shouldn't even let you come back to see me," she said. "Where are you staying?"

I told her.

"Mrs. Moore—hm, yes—I remember her. She's been ailing, hasn't she? She's not more than sixty-two or three, but her health has been failing. I haven't seen her for a long time, but that's what I hear."

I sat down.

"Say, you don't expect me to sit here and talk to you? Why don't you go over there and write about Mrs. Moore?"

"I'm sorry I rushed out last night," I said. "I was restless—couldn't sleep and seemed to hear noises . . ."

She watched me closely. Her lips began to twitch as if she could no longer keep back laughter over my crestfallen aspect.

"You were afraid," she said. "A noise! It takes me back to the time Mr. Wolfe thought he heard a burglar and asked me to go ahead of him . . .

"It was not long after we were married. In the dining room we kept the table set, and I heard something in the dining room that night rattling like dishes, and I said, 'There's somebody in the dining room. What are you going to do about it?' And he said, 'I haven't got anything to shoot with.'

"He called out, 'Who's there?' Nobody answered. I opened the door and didn't see anybody. We had a lamp in there then. We could see there wasn't anybody in the room. I said, 'The hall door's open and they have gone upstairs.' Mr. Wolfe said, 'We'll have to go up and see. You go ahead and I'll follow along and we'll find them in short order.'

"I said, 'All right, I have got a pair of scissors, and if I see him I will do like the story I read, jab the scissors in his stomach.' The stairs were the kind that went up in a winding, and there was a little offset right at the top of the stairs between the wall. Mr. Wolfe was behind me and we were hunting the burglar, and then, 'Meouw!' The old cat was in that corner. I said, 'There's your burglar.' And I said, 'Now, aren't you a brave one!'

"It was always that way in the case of an emergency. I think sometimes I was afraid, but I would go ahead and act anyhow. That is the difference between people. Like the time when Tom was a small boy, I guess about twelve years old, he was out tossing up a ball. I guess the ball was pretty heavy. Anyway, he came running in the house crying, 'Mamma, Mamma, I broke my finger.'

"Well, that middle finger, the joint was sticking out this way. I took hold of his hand—it was in the kitchen, and Mr. Wolfe was in there, and he went to the back porch. He said, 'I'm going to call the doctor.' I said, 'Just wait a minute.' I put his hand in a sauce pan of water, but I still had my hand tight over his finger, and I reached for a cloth with my other hand.

" 'Wait a minute,' I said, 'I will fix it all right.' And I got a strip of cloth and wrapped it tight around the finger in the water and gave it a jerk and back it went. Tom was so relieved, he kept saying, 'Oh, it's back, it's back all right.' And I said, 'Yes, it's all right now.'

"Mr. Wolfe had never said a word. I said, 'Now wouldn't you be a pretty mess in a severe case! Why, you would have sent for a doctor instead of acting.' And he said, 'Well, of course you can do it, you can do it.' Well, I wrapped something around it then. It swelled up a little bit, but in a day or two it was all right."

Chapter Six

One fine sunny Sunday afternoon I drove with Mrs. Wolfe several miles outside the city of Asheville, to the countryside of her childhood and young girlhood. We planned the trip several days earlier, when Mrs. Wolfe expressed a wish to find the forgotten resting place of her little brother, Sam, so she could snatch the long-dead boy from oblivion by purchasing a stone.

Before starting out, we stopped at a restaurant on the Square. Looking over the menu, it turned out neither of us was particularly hungry. We ordered soup, chicken soup, watery and yellow with patches of butter-grease floating on it. The crackers that were left she dropped into her purse. She spoke about the War Bonds she was carrying in her purse.

We left the town and, some miles out, drove along the little stream known as the Swannanoa River. Mrs. Wolfe was in a jolly mood.

"You know, I'd like to write about my life," she said. "I know everything that happened every year. I guess if I was like Tom I could paint it all up and tell a good many things. We moved about from one place to another. Father lived in Yancey County the first four years after they married. Henry and Sam were born there. They moved to Swannanoa and lived in a rented place and my sister, two and one-half years older than I was, was born there.

"My first memories are when I was a little over two years old. I remember everything that happened at the other places we lived. We lived at the Wilson place—it had a kind of sloped hill, and that is where I saw some of Sherman's army that passed. We lived there, and the Wilsons had built them another place down farther. And I remember their square garden, all picketed around, and I said, 'Oh, Mrs. Wilson, can I have one of those onions?' It was in the spring of the year, and they were just about that high, prettiest green onions, and she said, 'That's garlic, not onions.'

"Father bought a hundred acres a mile and a half or maybe two miles from there, up on the Swannanoa, from Mr. Burgin, and he built a home and Mother was happy. That's the place where we had the mountain field, and there was a kind of ridge where they built the house, and the finest huckleberries you ever saw growing, so many of them all over this ridge. I wanted to stay outdoors all the time . . .

"Father wasn't much of a farmer, but Henry had a horse to plow, and he had planted that mountain field, and he took Jim with him, a little fellow, to hoe corn, and he said, 'Now Julia will have to go with him—Jim

112

won't do a thing if she isn't along—just stand and gaze on his hoe handle.' "

Driving along the Swannanoa River, she remarked, "Now this is ugly, but it was beautiful when I lived out here, all grown up with trees and rhododendron and laurel and everything beautiful all around. Nobody lived along here—it was just bottom land. Trees—sycamore, white oak, black chestnut, poplars, maples, water birch, the pines, the black walnuts, the old hemlock.

"I was fifteen years old when we moved here. Father got a place up in town, but when we lived here we would walk to Asheville . . . I wonder if Charles Dickens died at that time? Back over the hollow there was a place you could cut off and it was shorter to Asheville. A great many people went up by our house to use the short cut. Well, brother Henry wasn't at home, but he had left an old suit there. I dressed up in Henry's clothes, combed my hair back, and went on up like I was going through. Then I came back and called, 'Did you know Charles Dickens was dead?' And say, they looked like they didn't know who I was. But I had to laugh, and then they knew I was dressed up in Henry's clothes and playing off. Perhaps Dickens had just died and Father had had the newspaper.

"You don't know what the primitive days were. If you got a newspaper once a week, you were lucky. There were no books, no schools unless they were private schools, and five or six miles to walk."

She asked me to stop the automobile.

"That's the house—the same house except they have made a hip roof now. It used to have a flat-top roof before, covered with tin. That house doesn't look as large to me as it did then. You know, that house must be a hundred years old . . . It was when we lived there that I used to dress up. I had a cousin from Yancey County—she was older than I—and we were up to mischief. She got one of mother's dresses and I dressed up in Henry's clothes, and we went out the back door and down the hollow and came up to the front porch and knocked—it must have been eight or nine o'clock at night. We had made up that we were traveling. Father said, 'What was it you said?' And I said we wanted a night's lodging. Then I just laughed and he slammed the door and went on. Mother said, 'What was it?' and he said, 'Oh, those fool girls.' He told Mother afterwards, 'She could fool you. She looked exactly like a young man if she hadn't laughed.' But I laughed and ran down the front steps. I couldn't stand it . . . But that's the same house.

"There was just a rocky road through here when I lived here, just wide enough for horse and buggy. The river was larger. Half of the water has been turned into different channels. It's not as wide. It looks like a branch to what it used to. We had a cloud burst, and Mother said, 'Get up and see the river.' The river was all the way out over that bottom, and way up here. You could see houses and pieces of things going down, and Mother said, 'Cheeseborough's house is washed out—

I've seen the lumber and all.' Then the bridge went, and they were in pretty bad shape. The boys slept out in the cabin, and they said the water was just under their arms when they got out. Father built them a new bridge—he was a contractor and builder. I suppose it is still there. Just a foot bridge, but wide enough so they could bring their carriage across. It was a hideous sight —it was a moonlight night, and the rain had stopped, and the river flowing down."

I drove on, and she spoke about her people, way back:

"Well, as they say, I'm Tar Heel born and Tar Heel bred, and when I die, I'll be Tar Heel dead. At one time there wasn't anything but Indians. But they kept on coming. The Alexanders and the Pattons, good stock of people, they came in. The Davidsons, Fosters, Alexanders, Pattons, Penlands, they peopled up this part of the country, and nearly everybody was kin. The first Westall that came to this country came with an English company. Mother said they were looking for copper, but I think it was gold. We had a box of those rocks at home—we played with them, and called them our gold rocks. They were the heaviest things, dirty-looking black like black lead, and those great big specks, some of them as big as little peas.

"William Westall was the first Westall who came over here. He went back to England and they said he was lost at sea. The only son was named William— Billy Westall. Grandfather's people are buried up at

Swannanoa, and as I say, brother Sam is still there. That was seventy-nine years ago, but I think I can find where he is buried. They called it the Patton grave-yard. I haven't been there for years . . .

"Say, I'll tell you about an old colored man—old Jason—who used to live in a cabin over there . . . He said that night of the cloudburst he had taken his axe into the room and put it under his bed, and that the water was clear up to his bed and what woke him was a dog up under the house barking. He reached out and got his axe from under the bed and cut his way out the back. It might have been true, but the dog couldn't have been under the house barking. Father went out through the woods to see if Jason was all right, and you could see the water was up by the house. The dog couldn't have been up under the house.

"The trees have been cut out since we lived here. It was more of a dense forest, but there was a pathway. We lived over there, and over the hill we had a garden. The garden was fenced in, but there were two planks knocked off the fence and not nailed up. It was winter time, and Father was coming across, and he thought old Jason was a good honest negro, but he saw him slip along and take those two planks and put them on his shoulder.

"Father was close by, and he came along behind him. He said, 'Jason, put those planks right back where you got them.' It scared Jason so he dropped down on

116

his knees. 'Oh, Major, forgive me—I'll never do anything like that again—forgive me this time.'

"Father said, 'I might forgive you, but I thought you were an honest man.' 'Oh, forget it, forget it,' Jason said. Father said, 'No, the confidence I once had in you will never be restored. You may never steal again, but I will always remember that you took those planks.'

"I went off and cried, and I thought it was awful that you couldn't restore your confidence in things. If anybody had asked Father before that, he would have said, 'Yes, Jason is an honest darky.' But after that he would always say, 'Jason stole the planks, and I don't know what he might do.' "

Mrs. Wolfe thrust out a hand suddenly: "There's Lover's bridge. I used to come out here and sit on the bridge. I didn't sit out here alone—I hoed two rows of corn at a time. I lived the outdoor life and liked company. You know, when I was a girl I don't think any girls cared much for me—but I never saw a man, young or old, but I got along with him. There wasn't an old widower in the county but what he was coming around. Some of them wanted to ask my father. And the young men would tease me about them. Well, I didn't go alone with the boys until I was about seventeen or eighteen, but I made up for it afterwards . . .

"See those pines—they were more beautiful then. It was the Murphy place—they had an open court all built of brick, and up above it was the slave house place. There was a nice driveway went around. That isn't the same house, the other one was all brick . . .

"There's the Cheeseborough bridge. I don't know whether that's the one that Father built or not, but he built the one after it was washed away.

"Oh, those old days. People would go out and shoot wild turkey and squirrels most any time. They had an easy life, didn't have to work much, didn't have to dress much, nowhere to go. I heard Father tell about a man over there, old Davey Ballew; of course, it was the custom then, wherever they would go they used to stop for dinner and stay overnight. He said he told him to 'take some more bear sop and a dash of taters.' Father would tell about it.

"Father played the flute. When he was a boy, a young man in the country went away and brought back a wife. You couldn't expect people to be anything but ignorant then—there were no schools. Anyhow, they sent for Father to bring his flute over and play for the bride. He went over and played all the pieces he knew, just kept on. She would sit and rock and rock, and finally when he had wound up, played until he was tired, she said, 'Well Mister, I reckon you could almost play a tune on that air thing.'

"Here's where Governor Craig lived—right in here. I initiated him in the temperance union, and he is the only one that kept the pledge. This looks familiar. There's the old Patton place, but they rebuilt it and it's the Ambler sanitarium. Dr. Ambler told Fred, 'I'm going over to see your mother—there are lots of things in Tom's book that happened long before Tom was born. Your mother is responsible for them. It's queer he didn't put me in the book.' Fred says, 'Look out, he may put you in the next one.'

"Cash Gudger was so glad he was in the book. What is it about Cash Gudger and one of the Redwood boys? Anyway, he was tickled to death. Tom made fun of them running around with the young girls when they were old enough to be their fathers. He said, 'Tom is the greatest man this country ever produced.' And he gets glory out of having ordered Tom's monument . . .

"My great-grandfather Patton owned most of the land all up the river, and my grandmother married a Penland, a man who carried a gun—not a well-to-do man. Grandmother wasn't quite sixteen years old, and he stole her and they ran away, and her father never spoke to them. But her mother sent her two of her slave women to cook and help keep house and wait on the children. So she didn't have such a bad time."

We passed a fellow and a girl loitering along the highway in the sunshine and smoking.

"I think the girls have lowered their dignity," said Mrs. Wolfe. "I don't think the men really appreciate them like they used to. When they drink and smoke just like the men do—why, they have got so they just go right in and take drinks with the men. I saw them in Brooklyn at Poor Richard's Corner. You come in to the lobby at the Franklin Arms Hotel and go into Poor Richard's Corner. And most of them come in and march right in. I went in there one time—Jane Stokely and I went in and took a lemonade, that's all we took. But most of them have highballs or martinis. Mr. Perkins, that is his drink, a martini.

"I went to the Vanderbilt Hotel with Mr. Aswell for lunch. He said, 'You'll take sherry?' and I said, 'Yes.' Just a small glass. But I noticed he would take the second martini. He would say, 'You prefer wine?' and I said, 'Yes, I'll take some sherry.'

"But there was a time, all my married life with Mr. Wolfe, I wouldn't have any more taken a drop of whiskey—never thought of such a thing. I was younger then, and I was a teetotaler. I joined the temperance order way back when I was a girl. They established the Sons of Temperance about 1882, and I was up there. Girls, women, men and boys, all joined up. So I went up Tuesday night and joined the league, and that night Squire Summey, one of the old aristocrats—he said they needed a worthy associate. That was something they had never put a woman in. So he popped up and said, 'I nominate Miss Julia Westall as worthy associate.' And Mr. Justice said, 'I second the motion.' And a lot of them said, 'Let's save time.' That is, elect you by acclamation, so they put you right in.

"But oh, didn't the girls hate me. They pretended to love me, though. Well, every three or four months when they had to have a worthy associate, I was re-elected.

They had the pledge all on a card and would come down to the altar and read it when they joined, and I thought I would take that card home and not have to read it, but would go down there and deliver it like a lecture, and they thought that was something extra.

"I was a strict temperance person. I put something in the water to make it look like wine, and I poured it out of the pitcher and said, 'Look not upon the wine that biteth like an adder and stingeth like a serpent,' and I went through the whole thing.

"One night there was a crowd and one of those girls who pretended to be my friend said, 'They think she is fine and pretty and all that—stick her up there for everything,' and another girl said, 'Sh-h-h.' Will, my brother, was sitting in front of them, and he turned around and said, 'I wonder why they don't put you up for something,' and got up and moved his seat.

"But I was a teetotaler then. I fought against tobacco and whiskey. Don't know whether I helped the country any or not, but I kept it up . . ."

She peered right and left as I drove slowly up the road.

"Uncle Bob Patton used to live somewhere here. Two stragglers from Sherman's army jumped the spring back there and went up the mountain. This has all been filled in. There wasn't any railroad there then. Right around this bend we lived, up around this branch. There was an old winding road. They rebuilt this road last year. The old road was down where the railroad is . . .

"Say, there is the old house where I was born! They have moved it back. They rolled it back, somebody told me. They widened this road and cut off most of the front yard, and the big old pine that stood out in the front is gone. And there were fruit trees back there. All back there was kind of a field, and nothing else in the world but a thicket. I wasn't old enough to remember living here the first time. We moved from here down to the old Trescott place, and Father built a home and then sold it, and when I was twelve years old Father bought this place and we lived here. I don't think we lived here more than three years. I came through here a few years ago, and it hadn't been changed. Mabel said, 'Why don't you buy that place now?' I could have bought it . . .

"Say, I'll tell you a story—there was a branch down here. Right along the old wagon road. The wagons went to Old Fort, that was the head road—the railroad came that far. So all the merchants sent their wagons here to get their goods. Out at Fletcher old Dr. Fletcher had a store. He was a respectable country doctor, and he would send his wagon.

"I knew Fletcher's wagon. The boy that drove it was a nephew of Dr. Fletcher's, eighteen or nineteen years old. He was the one who drove the wagon to Old Fort and back for the goods. I had been down to the Patton's, and I remember coming back and walking right behind that wagon. That must have been Friday. Sunday morning I went to Sunday school. It was a bright

Sunday morning, and I heard the tramp of horses over the rocks. The wagon was coming down that hill yonder, right after they crossed the branch. It woke me and I peeped out. It was just at sunrise. I looked out and it was Fletcher's wagon. I wondered where he camped. I remember all those things—about him driving along, and thinking he must have camped somewhere nearby.

"Maybe eight or nine days after that the whole country was excited. There had been a man murdered and cut up near Alexander's just outside of Black Mountain. Somewhere beyond there is where he camped by the river. They traced it down at Old Fort. He was a New York man who came south, a mineralogist. He'd had about $300 on his person. They found he had left with somebody driving—didn't wait for the train. The driver said, 'Yes, get up. You can go with me if you don't mind camping out.' Somebody had heard the driver say that.

"Well, they had gotten that far the first day—quite a distance. So they traced it down to that boy. That boy had murdered him and confessed the whole thing. But they never found the money. He told that he buried it out somewhere between Asheville and Fletcher in the woods. They got the gold watch, though.

"You know, that was a terrible thing for old Dr. Fletcher. People said likely he had turned over the money to Dr. Fletcher. But he was hung—they hung that boy. He confessed that after the man went to sleep he hit him in the head with an axe and then cut him up. He had put rocks on him, and about the ninth day he had come loose from the rocks and the dogs were barking and they found him. An old crazy man came along—his name was Smith, and he said, 'Be sure your sins will find you out.' Well, we are commanded in the Bible to watch and pray, and watch comes first."

Suddenly she saw a familiar landmark.

"You see those pines. That's where Father bought the one hundred acres and set those eleven pines out and three cedars. I helped put those pines out. Father dug the holes and the little kids put rocks on the roots to hold them in place and brought water and poured it in on them. There wasn't a pine that died, and ever since then I can put anything in the ground and it will grow if it has the least bit of life about it. I guess I learned it from Father.

"That is the place over there—but the house burned. This is that mountain, and that flat looks like it is all grown up in weeds again. That is where I planted all the seeds. These mountains were in the primitive state. There were minerals and all kinds of plants. Father had a book on botany, and we would take that book with us to the mountains, and we learned every plant from the pictures. There was different colored snake root and jimson—they called it sang . . . But my children grew up and didn't know any of that.

"There were plenty of apples here then. Say, Jim and I would stand out there at the gate at this place, and late in the evening the whole heaven looked like it was covered with birds in the fall of the year. I would say, 'They are going south for the winter.' But I don't see those flocks of birds any more. I read some time ago that the bird life had been killed out and they were trying now to preserve the forests . . . Brother Henry would tramp all around, hunting . . ."

She went on to speak of Henry, Thomas Wolfe's Uncle Bascom:

"He was eighty-eight the fifteenth day of January. He never did look like he had any flesh on his bones. He was tall, angular, over six feet. Tom pictured him pretty well. He was a boy brought up over here in the mountains with no outlets, and he went to Asheville to old Judge Bailey's law school. Henry was going to be the lawyer. When they finished they would have to go to Raleigh to stand an examination. Father spoke to him about it, and I remember how his eyes flashed. He said, 'Of course, you will have to have money to make the trip.' Henry said, 'I've decided not to go. I'm going north and get an education and be a minister.'

" 'What did you study law for then, if that was your idea?' Father asked. 'I don't think I've lost anything studying law, but I'm going first to get an education,' he said. He was a good student, but had no common sense. Grandmother said, 'You're smart in books and all that, but you have no common sense.' She was right. But they managed to get up the money and let him go.

"There was a college outside of Boston, and he had

written to the president—his name was Elmer Chapin. Elmer was born after that and he was named after that president. Mr. Chapin seemed to be sorry for Henry and he said, 'In this climate you will have to have a heavier overcoat.' The ministers got their tuition free, but had to pay for board and clothes. Chapin paid his board.

"That was a Universalist college. He was going to be a Universalist preacher. Henry started out as a Presbyterian, but Father had broken away from the church. Well, Henry didn't resign, he could get his tuition by being a Universalist. He stayed two years and then he went to Harvard, which was Unitarian. He preached for the Universalists a while and then was Unitarian. He took a theology course in his fifth year.

"He is well educated, and when he came home on a visit before I was married he preached all the way down and made enough money to make his way. Too proud to beg, and too honest to steal—his money ran out and there was some station where he had to stay over thirty-six hours, and he wrote home that pitiful story. And I remember Mother crying and talking on about it. He painted it all up, you know, and I said, 'Why didn't he ask somebody for something?'

"When Henry came back, he didn't talk like he had when he left home. I told him, 'You talk more like a Yankee than a Yankee himself,' and he does to this day. He was very precise. I said, 'When I make a mistake,

The Marble Man's Wife

Sept, 1947

Pathfon

Martin

Sampson

Hendricks

Stewart

Davenport

you need not correct me. I just talk in the old way.'
But he had forgotten the old way of talking.

"He didn't read 'Look Homeward, Angel' at first, he
didn't have one, and it was two or three years after it
was published that he said he made up his mind he
would get the book and read it, and he said, 'It's not
bad—not bad at all.'

"You know, Tom was his protege when he went to
Harvard. Laura would have him come over to dinner
and she treated him nicely. It was so lonely and far
away from home. At Christmas she would have him. I
found some of her letters—'Now Tom, be sure to be
here.'

"I wrote Tom one time to come on back. The people
have changed, but the hills and the mountains are the
same."

She directed, or rather misdirected the way, for she
was not sure, and after going up and down various
roads, we arrived at last at an unkempt rural cemetery.
We got out of the car and she went about looking for
Sam's grave. Little or no grass grew on the red-dirt
mounds. The withered and decaying cut-flowers on
fresh graves added to the gruesome aspect of the place.

She read the names on markers, and nodded, plucking at her lips. She remembered. The letters and dates
on the sagging stones of older graves unlocked neglected compartments in her mind.

I do not know by what by-way of the mind she came

upon the story of her one true love, but she stood in that acre of old and new grief and told about it:

"Well, he is dead," she said. "I always felt I was the guilty party. He got jealous over another man—a man I didn't care anything for. He got jealous of this one-armed Irishman who was crazy over me.

"What is it?—love at first sight? There's something in it, you can't tell what. Well, this Irishman, they said, 'He is a fool about you—you ought to marry that one-armed man.' I said, 'I'm not thinking about marrying.'

"And I went to this singing-school. We had a buggy. Brother Jim was going to drive me out, and Tom Reed and his sister Lula were riding horseback. Tom would ride with me in the buggy for a while, and then we would swap off with Lula and Jim and go horseback. Tom wanted to be a beau of mine, too. We got to Cane Creek, and there was this young man carrying a little grip. I didn't pay any attention to him till we got up with him. I said to Tom, 'Ask him to put his grip in the back end of our buggy, and we'll carry it.'

"He said, 'It's your buggy and horse, you ask him.' I begged him, but he wouldn't. I thought when we got up even with the man he would ask him. I said, 'You're the meanest thing.' Tom said, 'I believe you are in love with him.' I said, 'I never saw him before. What's the matter? He would think it very bold for me to ask him.' Tom said, 'I'm getting jealous right now.'

"Well, we went on and stopped at some people's for dinner, and I don't know what became of the young man. The next morning I didn't know anybody at that school but John Freeman and Mollie. It was in a Baptist church. We were up front, Lula and Mollie Freeman and I. Mollie and I sang soprano, and Lula alto. There was a kind of diagonal seat over there, and we could look across at John. John sang bass. I would look across at John and exchange glances and smile.

"On Wednesday before noon—we would take our lunch with us and stay there all day long until four o'clock in the evening—I sat in between Lula and Mollie. Mollie said, 'I'm going to lose my partner.' I said, 'What's the matter?'

" 'Oh,' she said, 'there's a young man here who hasn't taken his eyes off you.' Of course that excited me a little bit. I said, 'Where?' She said, 'If you promise not to look until I can get his eyes off you, I'll tell you where he sits. He hasn't had his eyes off you since Monday morning. Don't you look.' Just then he turned around to look out the front door, and she said, 'Look now.' I looked over there and there he was.

"I forgot I was staring at the man. And he turned back and I was looking at him. I reckon I stared and my stare was so that he dropped his eyes. I whispered, 'You mean to say he's been there ever since Monday morning?' And this was Wednesday. I had never seen him till she pointed him out—and it was the same man who carried the grip. It was just my sympathy because he was carrying the grip, and some kind of magnetism.

"Back in those days they didn't introduce anybody

—you had to get acquainted the best way you could. There was a song book we had bought when Professor Bowman was there. Judson Freeman had a fine voice, could sing alto, and this other one sang tenor. I said, 'Here's a good one—Jim and I have practiced this. Let's run over that—I can sing the soprano. We'll surprise Professor Chase—if I can just get somebody to sing bass.'

"I had my mind on this young man. I said, 'If I can just get somebody,' and I started down to the big old stove, when he stepped up to the church door, and I said, 'Mister, can you sing bass?' He was all smiles. I said, 'Oh, it will be easy. We are going to surprise Professor Chase. I'll take the lead.' We got up there, the four of us, and we hadn't sung but one verse when Professor Chase came in applauding and tapped the bell and they all came in, and he said, 'Just stand right there and we'll see how my folks have progressed.' Well, we sang it through, another verse or two, and Professor Chase stood there, nodding, nodding.

"This young man boarded a half mile nearer the school than Dr. Freeman's where I stayed. He went with me home every evening and came every morning to walk down with me the balance of the four weeks that singing-school lasted. That was the happiest four weeks of my life. I was about nineteen years old. Let me tell you, of all the people I ever went with, I liked him the best. I could put him down as a perfect gentleman.

"And he got jealous of this one-armed Irishman. He quit school when this man came out there. Old Professor McCarthy gave the Irishman too much liberty because he thought he was an older man—thought it was all right for him to go down town with me and take me to church. And he had no more religion than a rat. Professor McCarthy gave him privileges but didn't give any other young men privileges. And of course this man got so jealous. He said all my affections were centered in Mr. Davidson. He said I was a flirt, flatterer, and a deceiver. That hurt my pride. He left.

"That day he came back to get the balance of his clothes at the old Judson College, and he told Mrs. Morris, 'Don't tell her I was here and see what affect it will have on her. Tell her I hung myself.' Out at the graveyard at Fletcher he climbed a tree in the graveyard. He said something seemed to tell him he had better not jump. They thought it was a joke—they told me, 'He didn't mean a word of it—he thought you would get down on your knees to him.' I said, 'I haven't done anything.' They encouraged me by talking that way. If they had had more sympathy for the poor fellow. . . . He married long after I married . . .

"I told Mr. Wolfe when he insisted about marrying him, I told him, 'I have had a love affair, and I won't love anybody else like I loved him.' He didn't believe that. He thought you could learn to love. Mr. Wolfe's idea was to marry and learn to love afterwards.

"Well, there are a lot of things that people can do.

You can be very much attached to people and fight for each other and all that, go right through and live a happy congenial life. Good pals and friends, without any great love . . .

"That young man taught school. He was ambitious. He became a merchant afterwards. A man shot him—some man who'd been drinking. They were building a Presbyterian church, and he was treasurer of the fund, and the man came to explain about the lumber. They were out talking, and this drunk man came around the corner and shot him because he had refused him credit in the store. He didn't die right away—why, they thought he was going to be all right. But pus formed and caused peritonitis. The post-mortem showed it.

"Mr. Wolfe came home and I was upstairs making up my bed. It was about ten o'clock in the morning, and he came in and said, 'I have another name on my book.' He opened the book and there I saw the name. I said, 'What do you mean?' He said, 'He's dead.'

"Well, I had always thought that some time I would like him to know that I wasn't a flirt, flatterer and deceiver. It was too late now. And you know, I never saw his mother, but I dreamed she was telling me a short while after he died—I said, 'Where was he shot?' She said, 'Right through the lower part of the lung, and the bullet went out the back on the right side.' I hadn't heard anything about where he was shot, but that was exactly where it was.

"His wife came and spent two days and brought that little boy. She came to Mrs. Jim Gudger's—a friend of hers—and I invited her and she came. At dinner time— Fred and Effie were good-sized children—Mr. Wolfe joked. He said, 'Tell your husband that I'll swap with him now and give him two children to boot.' She was a good-looking, black-eyed woman and he married her and lived in Marshall . . . Well, where there is no love, there is no jealousy. A woman came here to stay and she said to Mr. Wolfe, 'She speaks to everybody uptown—it's a wonder you don't get jealous.' And he said, 'I wouldn't have a wife that nobody cared for.' I don't know—maybe you get immune to things."

The afternoon was wearing away and we returned to the automobile. She said she intended to come back some day and search further for Sam's grave. Perhaps it was in another cemetery, she wasn't sure.

"Don't drive fast," she said. "These roads and hills bring things back. The country quiet—brings back when Sally and I were girls we would get up and cook the breakfast in silence, and Father called it the 'Old Granny Swann.' I would set the table and make the coffee—and we wouldn't say one word to each other."

She told about her school-teaching days:

"They were afraid I would have trouble with the children—the Davis children were called the meanest children in the county. Afraid I couldn't manage. But I wrote down all the rules they were to abide by and tacked them up by the side of the window right above my head, and every morning when I went in I would read the rules out and say, 'Now, don't forget anything that is up there.'

"They had some new seats in the school, and one of the rules was that there was to be no marking or whittling on those seats. Well, I was teaching and rip—rip —rip. I looked over and Jim Davis had a knife out and was cutting right down the back of the seat in front of him. I said, 'You go over there and stand in the corner —turn your back and look at the wall until I finish with this class.'

"He didn't go, and I said, 'Jim, aren't you going to do what I tell you to do?' 'No,' he said, 'not going to do it.' I said, 'Yes, you will. I'll give you five minutes to do it, and if you don't, I'll give you a switching.' You could have heard a pin fall. I said, 'Wes, go out there and cut me a sprout.'

"Now, I thought Jim would go, but he didn't. The switch was brought in—it wasn't much of a switch. The five minutes was out and I walked right down to that boy and gave him a few cuts. He didn't feel it, but it was the humiliation. I finished the lesson and said, 'Everyone go get your lunch.' I went out and Jim was sitting on a stump in the yard, just boohooing. I went up and put my arm around him and said, 'But you see, you must obey. If you had gone directly as I told you, I wouldn't have had the switch brought in, but I had to carry out my word. Go on down there and wash your face in the creek and have your lunch.'

"When we got home that evening, Wesley had to tell it. He said, 'Well, Miss Julia had to thrash Jim Davis today,' and Mr. Bailey looked worried, and he said, 'If old man Davis comes up there, you send for me.' And I said, 'I won't have any trouble.'

"Well, the first people I saw in the school yard in the morning were the Davis children, and the little girl had a note and ran to meet me and said, 'Papa sent you a note—Papa almost wore him out when he came home and he says for you to give him another.' I read the note. He said, 'If one of my children disobeys don't hesitate to give them a thrashing and I will give them another one.' Well, you never saw a better boy after that than Jim. I never had any trouble with any of them again.

"And I taught for three years. We got married the fourteenth of January and I said to Mr. Wolfe, 'I promised to go to Swannanoa to teach this year—they're expecting me the first of February. I could come home every Friday evening and stay through Sunday.' He said, 'What did I marry you for?' I said, 'Where am I going to get any money?' He said, 'If I can't make money enough to keep us both, I had no business getting married.'

" 'Well,' I said, 'I'm too independent to ask for money, I never liked to ask Father or Mother.' But he said no, so I didn't go, and I reckon it was just as well.

We had three extra rooms down home, and Asheville didn't have any hotels. I went down to one of my old friends at the post office, he was the registry clerk, and I said, 'I'm cooking for myself and Mr. Wolfe, and can't cook little enough. Don't you want to come down and board?' He said yes, and brought two other young men down for meals. Summer came on and tourists came in and Mr. Barnard wanted me to take two friends of his from Danville, Virginia, and I took them. I wanted all I could accommodate, and I kept them filled up for the summer. I hired a cook to help me, and old Uncle did the chores and brought home what groceries Mr. Wolfe didn't bring in. All the money that was paid I handed over to Mr. Wolfe—never kept a dollar and boarded him, too. I wouldn't do it today, though . . .

"All those roomers and boarders I've seen come and go . . . Funny psychology, isn't it? Say, I'll tell you —when a man and wife come in and register, I don't pay any attention to them. Some of the others would see them go out and say, 'You reckon they are married? —Mrs. Wolfe, how can you tell?' Well, I'd say, 'When you see a man that doesn't pay any attention to her, they're always married.'

"And say, speaking of those people—I could live on Easy Street if I had what has skipped out on me. Often they paid me in advance for the first week or first few days, and they would stay on and on, and the first thing you knew, they were gone. That was a trick. They knew my habit, knew I wouldn't get up just with the birds, and they would go. Some of them got away with it."

"Wait a minute, boy—now stop the car."

I applied the brakes.

"I saw some dandelions back there," she said. "You know, I'd like a taste of dandelion greens. I'm going back there . . ."

She walked back to the side of the country lane, bent down and pinched off the young dandelion plants. She placed them in her purse, along with the soup crackers and the War Bonds.

She looked west, toward the declining sun, peering intently.

"Say, that hill—that road a-winding up. It brings back—I don't know . . . Makes me think . . .

"He was Father's friend—W. C. Bowman. Very intellectual, and had the same religious and high ideals of life that Father had. He went to California. Promised he would pick out a lot for us to build a house on out there in California somewhere in his neighborhood. Mr. Wolfe went to California in February—left here the twentieth of February. I sent him to pick us out a home and a place for his business. He sent me the literature from every place. I would read up and write ahead, 'Be sure to see so and so.' He would write back what a grand time he was having, and never say anything about business. By the time he got to San Francisco I had a letter there waiting for him. As he told some people when he got back, 'She certainly sent me a scorching letter. Said I was out for a good time and hadn't said anything about business.' I wrote him, 'Now since you have had a good time long enough, come back home and tend your business and let me tend my children.'

"Though Mr. Wolfe would work. He would often get three negroes and himself, and he would have to lift against the three negroes, and I said, 'What do you do it for?' and he said, 'They would drop it, and I can't afford to have anything chipped off.' The doctors thought maybe that was one cause of his trouble, lifting. He had good big hands. Long hands and long arms. Longer arms in proportion than Tom. He wouldn't buy anything unless he had it tailored. Towles Brothers in Baltimore made his shirts. He got half a dozen at a time. Way back in the olden days he paid $12 for six shirts. It was expensive in those days, but they were tailored shirts.

"Well, Mr. Wolfe left the twentieth of February. We went up to take the whole family group in a picture, and some of them moved and the photographer got mad. Mr. Wolfe said, 'Well, we'll just have ours taken together.' And he took that picture—the two of us—with him to California. He said, 'I think the old lady was jealous—Mrs. Bowman was jealous.'

"You see, Mr. Bowman held that picture about fifteen minutes, and Mr. Wolfe said he thought it made the old lady jealous. W. C. Bowman was a professor in the old Asheville Female College and a minister in the

Methodist Church at the end of the Civil War. When
I was a girl he came back here from Atlanta and he
tried to get this old Academy School. There was some
trouble and he didn't get it. When he left—I don't
know, there was something between us; I seemed to
have the same affection that I had for my father for

Walt Whitman, 1850.

the man because he was my
gentle sort of man. When he
cried, and he said, 'I'm com-
I'm coming back.' But he
Bowman went to New Mexico
fter to Los Angeles, and they
rresponded with him a long
lifornia, and I could tell alto write before I got the let-
I had a letter from him, and
fferent organizations printed,
between, and when the letter
wrote him and said, 'I read
f way out to California.' And
y—that there was a spiritual

he looked at the picture, and
ia,' and Mrs. Bowman said,
cture, I haven't seen the pic-
was jealous, Mr. Wolfe said,
d him about people there and
he wouldn't talk about anybody but Julia, and I asked
him if there wasn't anybody else back there but Julia.'

'Well,' I said, 'there's the whole neck of the United States between us.' "

We returned to the automobile for the ride back to Asheville. Mrs. Wolfe said, "Say, when I think about it—all those people who've stayed at my place—all walks of life as the saying goes, and all kinds . . .

"There was this woman came down here from the North. The people in the house didn't care for her. She would go over to the negro church, was interested in them. I had a colored man I got from Georgetown— that colored school—and he was studying law and brought his books along. I found him several times coming down from this woman's room, that big room over the living room, and I thought, 'He isn't cleaning up for her.'

"And he said, 'You know, she is helping me with my lessons, when I get through with my work.' He was a good servant and all that, but some of them found out that she was teaching that darky, and said she was a negro lover and she went over to the negro church. She had been a teacher in New York for years, and I said no, I didn't think I could put her out. We Southerners are bitter or narrow-minded about some things, but I told them I couldn't put her out. I said when Tom wrote the story I recognized that was the school teacher . . .

"And way back there, when Mabel's mother-in-law took sick—Mrs. Wheaton and her daughter Geraldine

came up to Mabel's wedding. They had just finished
building a home in Allendale, Florida, and were pretty
well worn-out. I had guests in the house and there was
a whole lot of work to do. I put Mrs. Wheaton with the
chicken salad, and she had a good appetite and ate so
much while she went along. The night of the wedding,
you know, everybody was helped bountifully. They
were all over the house and the porch. We helped her
twice with the chicken salad, and she had been eating
all day long.

"Mabel was fair and beautiful that night. She put off
her wedding dress and put on a blue dress and a hat
and everything that matched, and they said goodbye
and left—she and Ralph—they went to the Battery
Park Hotel and were going to leave next morning and
drive to Raleigh. Well, after it was all over, about
twelve o'clock, I said, 'Anybody want anything—ice
cream, cake, chicken salad? There's plenty of it in
there.'

"So I set everything out and said, 'Come out here
and everybody help themselves.' And Mrs. Wheaton
helped herself—it was twelve o'clock at night—and the
next morning I got up—didn't make any difference how
tired I was, I got up at six o'clock—and Geraldine
came in and said, 'Mother's been sick—awful sick for
hours. I don't know what in the world I'm going to do.
She's awful sick.'

"Well, I found she was very sick. I thought, 'The
old woman's going to die.' I went to the phone and told

Ralph, 'Better come and see your mother before you leave.' He came, and there was a niece of mine here who was a trained nurse but not taking cases, and I called her to come over. When she came, she told Ralph, 'You had better wait and not go—she's a sick woman.' Of course Ralph—his mother was all he had, though he had Mabel now—but he was very fond of his mother. They stayed, and the nurse waited on her all night long—had an electric grill to keep hot applications, and she said next morning, 'I hate to tell Ralph. She is going to die—we will have to take her to the hospital—we aren't equipped here to take care of her. You can't have her here in the house—the sheets and towels and everything would keep you busy.'

"So we sent her to the hospital, and I don't know how long she was over there. But she had will power. They brought that ambulance here and they had put on her hose but no shoes, and she roused up and said, 'Where are my shoes?' And they tried to tell her nobody would notice it, but, no sir, she wasn't going without them, and they finally had to put the shoes on. And she got well again after all. Tom wrote about it, the old lady getting so sick . . .

"About that time Tom was in Norfolk—he and this boy had drawn their money and they suggested, 'Let's pay the month's rent in advance,' when they went to get a place to stay. Afterwards Tom began thinking, 'We won't get paid off and we'll run out of money before our next payday.' They did run out, and they were hungry. They finally got in touch with Fred and Fred wrote it home. Ben was home that summer. I went into the dining room because I never liked for anyone to see me cry. When they told me about it I said, 'Why in the world didn't he telegraph for some money. We could have sent it to him.'

"Ben said, 'Cut out crying, he's all right now. Fred's taking care of him.' I said, 'It's an awful thing that he should go hungry when we've got loads of everything.' I sat down and wrote him a letter, and I said, 'Why in the world did you do such a thing?' It was poor judgment with them, paying the woman her big price for the whole month. He said they were hungry and they searched their pockets and found a dime in the lining and went out and bought a pie with it . . ."

Night had fallen when we reached town, and I parked the car before the Old Kentucky Home shadowy in the feeble gleam of the street light. I was hungry and my stomach murmured under my belt. I had suggested a restaurant, but Mrs. Wolfe had declined, saying she was going to cook herself a bite. She was speaking of her travels:

"Can't count how many times I've been to Washington and Florida. Twenty odd times to Florida, anyway. The first time I went to Washington was with Mr. Wolfe. It was after we had been married some time, but that was the first time we went north. We were going all the way to Boston, but I got sick at Philadelphia

and decided I wouldn't go on. Thought I would get out
with his people and get well, but I didn't. Went to Harrisburg, and came back home . . ."

She seemed reluctant to cease speaking and go into
the house, and I made bold to put her a few questions.
I asked her if it were true, as Wolfe wrote in "The
Web of Earth," that Cynthia had had a child.

"There's more truth than poetry in that," she replied
readily enough. "It was no living child. It was a prenatal child, and nobody knew anything about it. Cynthia was a milliner in Raleigh and went north to buy
goods and stopped in Washington. She didn't mean to
come back to Raleigh at all. The doctor told her to get
on back, that she had a tumor, and if she had a mother
to go back home. She got on the train and came home.
Mr. Wolfe's brother, Wesley, lived in Washington City
at that time, and he was still in Raleigh carrying on his
business. She left there and didn't expect to come back.
The old lady said she was packing up her things to go
away, and she had one of those mottoes worked with
floss or wool—'The Lord Will Provide'—and she gave
that picture all framed to her mother. She cried over it
when she was packing. And she went north never to
come back. But she came back to Raleigh. It was pretty
hard all the way round. She stopped off at Mebane,
North Carolina. The train stopped there. Wesley Wolfe
came that far with her, and they took her off the train,
and she came on into Raleigh next day . . ."

I said, "Mrs. Wolfe, you remember that scene on the

railroad platform in 'Of Time and the River,' where Eliza Gant said to Eugene, 'You think you're the youngest . . .' "

She made a little gesture. "Oh, I think Tom was trying to talk about everything else to keep from breaking down at the last minute. Robert Weaver was Henry Stevens. Henry committed suicide in New York. His grandmother died in the insane asylum. Some hereditary streak caused his breakdown . . ."

I went with her up the steps, up the cement walk leading to the porch. Halfway up the walk she paused, facing the house. Standing there near her, I felt on the moment that she had forgotten that I was there, and together we stood looking at the old rooming house buried in night.

Chapter Seven

I found Mrs. Wolfe a woman of inflexible determination. If she wanted to go somewhere, she went. If she didn't want to go, she stayed. Mayhap there were honeyed tongues able to sway her against her will, but I have no doubt that in her long life she encountered few such.

She was planning to pay a visit to Brooklyn and Manhattan at the time I left Asheville, and since my home was less than a hundred miles from New York, I suggested she make the trip with me. She refused. She was not ready. In a day or so, maybe a week, she said. But I could not wait. My money was nearly gone. With Mrs. Wolfe a day or a week meant nothing in terms of money. It was merely that she wasn't ready to go when I went. The arguments I thought most persuasive fell to the ground: the trip in the automobile through spring-green mountains and saving the expense of trainfare.

"It won't cost you a penny," I said.

But she was not ready. She was quite good-humored about it. She intruded on my begging several times

with a faint husky chuckle in the back of her throat.
She looked at me slyly as if she were only teasing and
I thought she might give in in a moment. But she was
firm.

"I tell you what," she said, "I can't come with you
to New York now, but I tell you what—I'll come to
see you in Bethlehem."

By what secret path of the mind she had reached
this decision, I do not know. But she had made up her
mind to come to Bethlehem, and come she did. Within
a month she sent me a card from Brooklyn. I called her
on the phone and she said, "Sure, come on up and I'll
ride back to Bethlehem."

"I'll come to Brooklyn this afternoon," I said.

"All right," she said. "All right, I'll see you then."

So I drove fast to Brooklyn, to the Franklin Arms
Hotel, and the bellhop put her bags in the car and we
drove back to Bethlehem. On the way a thunderstorm
developed.

"I am always afraid of lightning," she said, although
she appeared quite calm and at ease. "I don't know, I
read somewhere that lightning will not strike a moving
automobile . . . This takes me back, these bright
flashes—back to when I lived with the Bailey's at the
time I was teaching school near Spruce Pine, at the
Brush Creek schoolhouse. It was about half way between Spruce Pine and Flat Rock, that schoolhouse.
Well, I had finished the term and had to wait. There
was no transportation and I had to depend on friends.

Mr. Bailey was going over to Asheville in three or four weeks, and I stayed around and visited.

"I stayed around and visited, and then we rode horseback to Marion, twenty-four miles over the mountains, planning to stay the night with some friends of the Bailey's three miles outside of Marion, and take the morning train into Asheville. Pinckney would take the horses back . . . I was right on top of Little Switzerland that day. Little Switzerland was built just where I said, 'Wouldn't that be a fine place to build!' It was beautiful but lonely.

"It was very dark that day, making ready to storm. I was riding a black horse, a fine horse. We went Indian file, John Bailey up in front, and I between John and Pinckney.

"Suddenly a great crash of lightning struck a tree and the whole top went out. The flash blinded me and the horse jumped, and the tree fell down. It took the whole top off. John Bailey looked around, and I said, 'Let's go back to that house we passed.' I said, 'It might rain.' It was about a quarter mile back, and we went back, but it didn't rain and the storm passed by. That was a crash! The lightning and thunder right together. I came very near going that time. I was fairly stunned, and John said, 'Don't get scared, maybe we won't have another crash.' And he said, 'You looked awful white on that black horse.' I was twenty-two or twenty-three years old then.

"Well, we spent the night at the Pattons out from

Marion and got up early to take that train to Asheville.
I was never afraid of a train, but I will say I'm afraid
of lightning. I was younger then and nervous too . . . I
am going to tell you something that happened. I was
never afraid to ride on a train, but before the train
came up, and I heard the train coming, I said, 'Today
I am afraid. Something's going to happen on that train.'
Pinckney said, 'What's the matter, Miss Julia?' I said,
'I don't know. There's going to be a wreck or something on that train today.' They said, 'Oh, it's going to
be all right.' We took the train, said goodbye to Pinckney, and John and I came on. He was a kind of bachelor. Well, we hadn't gotten six miles out of Marion—
I kept on saying, 'There's something terrible going to
happen. You reckon the train will be wrecked?'

"And he laughed. 'What in the world, Miss Julia!
What's the matter with you?' We came on, and on top
of the mountain there was a place called Mud Cut. I
was sitting over on the side next the window, and John
sitting next to me. And it was just like we rolled over a
log. I said, 'Something's happened.' John said, 'Don't
get excited.' I said, 'Something terrible's happened.'
I stuck my head out and they were jumping out down
by the engine. John said, 'Don't worry, we are still on
the track.'

"Presently somebody came through and said they
had run over a man out there. It was just like you had
run over a log. It was the engineer trying to stop the
train. It was the signal master. You see, there were so

many turns and twists to go around, the engineer didn't have time to stop. The man was lying over the tracks and the train went over his body."

Mrs. Wolfe shook her head, a brief shuddering movement.

"I felt something was going to happen, just as soon as I heard that train. Dr. Skinner, an old aristocrat from Raleigh, was on the train, sitting diagonally across from us, and they eased the train on down after they got the body from underneath the wheels. Then they brought up one of those little hand cars. Dr. Skinner said, 'Don't look out; make you have bad dreams.' But you couldn't keep me from looking out. John Bailey said, 'There's nothing to it. He just looks like a man lying there.' The only thing I saw, of course, was that the man was dead. I just saw a little blood on his upper lip where it came out of his nose.

"He was a signal hand and he was drunk; had a bottle of liquor in his pocket. His family lived close to the track, in a cabin, and the conductor sent somebody to tell his wife before they brought the body there. They put a pin in that little hand car and coupled it on behind and put the body on that little car, and then they took the pin off and left him in front of the house, and the women and children and some other people, you could hear them screaming as we went on. John Newland was the conductor on that train. He looked pretty sad. Old Dr. Skinner gave the conductor a ten-dollar bill and said, 'Send this to the wife.' "

Mrs. Wolfe was silent, but only for a moment.

"That was one of the experiences I had going back and forth," she said. "Came very near being killed with lightning, and then had a tragedy on the same trip."

She broke into a little laugh, "Hah!"

"I was lightning proof, though," she said. "We had an argument. I was over at the old Judson College and Professor McCarthy had twin boys, Fred and Charlie, and they always tried to get in an argument about something with me. I was a giddy girl about eighteen or nineteen. They asked a question—why is it some people are more attractive than others. We were talking about people possessing magnetism. I said, 'It's just a form of electricity in their system.' They laughed at me. I said, 'I can prove that I'm a non-conductor of electricity, and we'll let Professor McCarthy decide the question. I'm a descendant of a family named Westall,' I told them, 'and way back a storm came up and struck a bed with two children in it. One was killed and the other wasn't. I'm a descendant of the one that stood the lightning. I possess more electricity than the ordinary person.' Well, it was foolish, but Professor McCarthy said, 'I believe she's got you there.'"

I drove rather slowly because of the heavy downpour, and we reached Bethlehem late at night. She commented on the ruddy hue off to the left, and I told her the steel mills were over there. She said she would like to go through a steel mill. "But I suppose they wouldn't allow me," she said, "because of the war."

I suggested that tomorrow we might take a ride along the road past the mills and look at them from the outside.

"Yes, yes," she said eagerly, "I'd like to see them."

My father was on the point of going to bed when we arrived. He was going on a business trip the next day, and he looked tired. Mrs. Wolfe shook hands with him, and he commented later on her firm grip. He spoke about the greatness of her son. He was embarrassed, trying to sound not too trite. What can one say when introduced to the mother of a genius? It is very difficult. I have seen a good many meet Mrs. Wolfe for the first time, and always she appeared self-possessed, rather pleased with herself in a quiet way, her lips pursing and unpursing themselves spasmodically sometimes. And sometimes she threw me a wink.

She sat in the parlor in a soft chair, and my dog, a Boston, inquired at her ankles. She scratched his ears gently. "You can always make friends with a dog," she said, "if you do like this . . . Like this. You know," she said, looking sharply at my father, "I knew there was a dog in the house the minute I stepped in. I could tell. I don't know as it was any smell—I don't know, but I could tell."

She told about Brute, a dog of her childhood: "He was white, a short-haired dog, white all over. I don't know how to describe the dog—we didn't go by brands.

I am sure what hounds were, but Brute wasn't a hound. He was just a big dog and had a kind of big face and a mean disposition.

"He would growl if you pointed your finger at him, and I don't know where they got such a word, but those brothers of mine—Will and Jim and Lee—would tease that dog, and he would go up under the part of the kitchen that was open, and they would get up under there where it was nice and cool in the summertime, and they would crick their finger at him and say, 'Zime Zuds' and make him so mad.

" 'Zime Zuds, Zime Zuds,' and crick their fingers at him, and oh he would growl. But he had a good disposition just the same. Oh, he was good to follow around, and he would not bite anybody. Maybe he thought everybody expected him to growl . . ."

"Mrs. Wolfe," I said, "I'll show you the way to the bathroom."

She looked at me; sitting there in the soft chair, she made no movement whatever, except a slight movement of the lips, her expression humorous. "Oh, I'll find it," she said.

In a little while I went myself to the bathroom, and when I returned to the parlor she was telling my father about her childhood:

"I might startle science if I say too much. I could read when I was three years old. My father taught me to read. But I can go farther back than that. When I was two years and four or five months old I could remember distinctly many things just the same as if it was yesterday.

"I was two years old the sixteenth day of February, and in June my two older brothers came in one day with those gallon buckets with the prettiest blackberries. I know how large they were! And the boys said, 'We have made Lewis Harris out of black clay.' Lewis and Alec were two black slave negroes that belonged to the Harris' and my sister and I were afraid of them. I remember they would come to the fence and laugh, and they knew we would run, and it tickled those two negroes.

"They were great black negroes with big white teeth and bright eyes—so black they had that black shine on them. Uncle George used to say a piece of charcoal would make a white mark on them. Well, when my brothers said they had made Lewis Harris down in the ditch with this black clay, Sally and I wanted to see it, yet we were afraid of it. The boys had got black clay from the spring branch, and they had taken this black clay and sticks and I remember now that black man lying there. I wouldn't go anywhere near him. So Henry picked me up and carried me across the branch. But I wouldn't go within ten feet of that black mud man. I knew he was mud, yet I was afraid of him. I was two years and four or five months old at that time. I remember distinctly how those boys looked with the buckets of berries."

There was a pause, and my father blinked his tired eyes. He said, "Henry—he was a brother? An uncle?"

"My brother Henry, the eldest," she replied. "Henry is six years, one month and one day older—that much ahead of me. Of course, he was old enough—children would go out and do work in those days. Sam was about two years younger; Sam was about seven years old at that time. Sam was seven years old the eleventh of September.

"But you mentioned Henry. He was dyspeptic, a student. He would study at night. He was thin; black eyes, black hair. He had some indigestion, that was the reason his disposition wasn't so sweet. I had it too when I was a girl. It didn't make any difference what you ate, it would come back in your throat sour. A lady told me what to do. She said she had read in some journal where if I would take two tablespoons of skimmed milk without cream every hour of the day, it would cure the worst forms. I didn't stick exactly to that, of course, but I cured it finally. Sometimes I would eat an apple, and that was all right, too. When I went to Judson College I still had some of it, especially if I ate anything that had too much grease, too rich. I boarded at Professor McCarthy's, and he would buy the old style square soda crackers in barrels. They had a cook and I said to her, 'If there are any burnt crackers, save them for me.' So Emma would hunt out the crackers and say, 'Miss Julia, look, I've got you some crackers.' And I would take them to my room and nibble on the brown crackers and it would cure those spells."

Mrs. Wolfe was silent now, all at once, absorbed in her thoughts. The dog slept near her crossed, swollen ankles, and snored slightly, but she did not appear to hear. She went on:

"That mud man—those boys with the berries . . . I remember several things that happened that year. The next winter—I don't know how I knew, but I had the feeling that Mother thought there was something going to happen when the stars were falling. There were millions of stars and it looked like the whole heaven was falling. It was on the north side of the house, and I was up in Father's arms and he was standing at the back door, and Mother cried, 'Oh, oh!' But nothing ever bothered Father. He knew it was just a natural consequence. You know, Mother used to be superstitious, and I remember she thought there was some great calamity coming when I said the stars were falling."

"What year was that?" my father asked.

"The winter of '62 or '63," Mrs. Wolfe replied. "You know, I am going to look it up some time and see if there was a meteor. I clung to Father. It was a meteor instead of stars, but it looked as if all the stars in the heavens were falling. I remember just how they looked as they went by.

"We lived at that place then. I can remember very well, because up until the time I was seven years old

Father didn't own a place. This was my aunt's place that they moved to, you know, so Aunt Myra and Mother would be together as her husband was in the War and with children it wasn't safe to be alone. We only lived there a year, because in February—the sixth of February—no, the tenth—just six days before I was three years old, my little brother Sam died. I suppose it was spinal meningitis. He was just sick one day. I remember the night he was sick, but I don't remember when he died. I guess I was baby enough to be put to bed early.

"He died that night about nine o'clock, and the next day they had the funeral and I didn't know why Sam didn't wake up. Aunt Hannah took us out near the house where there was a branch and a spout which they called 'the washing place,' and you had to put a bucket under that spout. Well, she took us down there to wash our faces, and Sally and I were with her, and I asked her then, 'What is the matter with Sam?'

"I knew there was something terrible wrong in the house. And she says, 'Sam's asleep.' Well, that afternoon they had some funeral services there at the house, and brother Jim was about seventeen months old and he could talk; he was the one next younger. Father was holding him up, and Sam was laid out in the trundle bed and smiling—a beautiful boy. And Jim says, 'Sam's smiling. Sam's smiling.' Jim don't remember anything about it. He is J. M. Westall, and he was eighty years old last September. I said, 'Jim, don't you remember that?' No, he said, he didn't remember Sam at all.

"Sam was Mother's. She felt nearer to him, and she couldn't live there any longer in that place, so we moved away from that place and went to the Davidson Mill place. While we lived at this place—it was in the fall—I remember we made a playhouse, and I remember the deer coming out of the thickets, and it had great antlers. When I screamed, that deer ran . . .

"I went by that place not long ago, the first time in fifty or sixty years, and I told Fred, 'There's the place I lived up to the time I was three years old.' I guess I was two or three when they moved there. No, three. I was three years old just after Sam died. Mother couldn't live there, and they moved, and while I was there—Father used to be a surveyor—and there was a man, I expect maybe Father surveyed land for him. I remember I was in Father's lap—I was always in his arms or lap until I was a great big girl, maybe eight or ten years old. I had climbed up into his lap; it was winter, I think—anyway cold enough for a fire. I climbed up in his lap, and Father said, 'Read for Mr. Clontz.' I always delighted in reading for people. So I read in my best manner, and I looked over there and my sister and brother Henry were laughing, and I was hurt and cried, and I said, 'I read that all right, but they are making fun of me.' And Father said, 'You read

it all right. They are laughing because you are reading
to a deaf and dumb man.'

"Well, I knew Mr. Clontz was deaf and dumb, and
it made me feel foolish, but he was sitting over there
and smiling and nodding, and Father said, 'Now, Mr.
Clontz says he understood every word of it. Now, don't
you worry, don't you cry. Mr. Clontz said he understood every word.'"

Mrs. Wolfe looked from me to my father with humorous shining eyes and tremulous lips, and my father
creased his tired features in a smile. He told Mrs.
Wolfe he had to leave early in the morning on a business trip, excused himself and went to bed.

Mrs. Wolfe inquired regarding my father's age, and
I told her he was about sixty. She remarked that it was
too bad he felt so tired. She remarked, blinking at me
humorously, that she was old enough to be his mother.

Chapter Eight

The next day my sister cooked a steak and it was tough. Mrs. Wolfe said mildly that she had encountered tough steaks before. She said in a disarmingly joking manner that the cow was old maybe, but not beyond hope. She pounded the steak with the butt of a butcher-knife, put it back on the stove for further cooking, and after that it was perfectly tender.

We went for a ride past the steel works. "This is ugly," Mrs. Wolfe said. "I don't like this. The smoke and dirt . . . You know, Mr. Wolfe came from Pennsylvania. He talked about the barns, the big red barns —they were better than the houses the people lived in. And I've seen them, too. Everything so fine and clean, and the fields and crops, and in the winter the crops stored away, the barns full. Mr. Wolfe used to tell about the farms in Pennsylvania—said we didn't know what farms were like, you know—and when we went north, I saw them myself."

I suggested a drive out into the countryside so she could see some nearby farms, and she said yes, yes, eagerly. She cast not a backward glance at the steel works.

We drove out into the Saucon Valley section, where Bethlehem Steel men had built themselves elaborate country homes on lush estates. Her thoughts turned to real estate:

"Mr. Wolfe did not want anything but a home and he would pay rent for his marble shop," she said. "He would not own a home either, except that he did not like to move. When I married Mr. Wolfe, he had this home, and he rented his marble shop. He did not pay very much rent and it was out of what he earned that I wanted him to buy a lot up in the building section of the town and build a business . . . Patton Avenue was about to spring up. I said to Mr. Wolfe, the traffic will be down there instead of on the Square. I said I wanted to be down there where traffic came by that way. I wanted a place where people came passing by. I said, 'We will not build just now. We will put all the money in a lot. We can build later on.'

"Well, I sold the house I had built on Chestnut Street and bought the lot and put the balance of the money—it sold for $1,600—in that marble shop. That way we got it. He was agent for the Chambers Iron Fence Company. He had to have some iron to put across for columns, and the Chambers Company sent him some for advertising, and he paid the freight on it. He got that free. The Georgia Marble Company sent him more blocks. He put that in front. He only had to pay the freight on that.

"We had to scheme to get that building without any debt left behind us. Mr. Wolfe was a pretty good trader. We got that building built and did not put much money on it. He got somebody to do the painting. They took that out in trade. He ordered a carload of marble, and the freight had to be paid. He had to borrow $700. He wanted that marble. I said, 'A mortgage eats while you sleep, we don't want anything with a mortgage on it.' He said, 'We have to have this. I can pay them out maybe in thirty days,' he said, 'but I have to have $700 to pay the freight off.'

"Mr. Wolfe told me some man wanted to loan $700 for a year. I said, 'Can you take it for six months?' I said, 'I won't eat or sleep with it hanging over.' I said, 'Mr. Wolfe, why don't you have a separate account in the bank and have $700 put in that account so that when six months is up, we can pay it off? As soon as you get $700 placed to that account, pay it off.'

"Well, one day he came home and said, 'Don't lose any more sleep and don't fail to eat'—oh, we had plenty to eat, I cooked it myself—but he said, 'I've put the money in the bank to pay off the mortgage, so go on and eat, don't worry any more.' And after that was paid off, there wasn't any debt on anything . . .

"We made a little money on two lots on Charlotte Street. I met an agent coming away from Mr. Wolfe. I said to this man—a fine man—I said, 'If you are selling that property, I want to buy it.' I said, 'Come back with me.' He said, 'I can't do anything for you, Mr. Wolfe doesn't want to buy.' Well, I said, 'Mr. Wolfe, why don't you buy those two lots out there?' He said, 'We don't want them.' I said, 'I know we can sell them and make $50 in a year's time.' I said, 'Your money is not at interest in the bank, just an open account will not get anything.'

"Well, the agent said, 'Mr. Wolfe, listen to her. I am selling the lots cheap.' It was $300. I said, 'Mr. Wolfe, if we don't sell it in a year's time, we will build two cottages, turn in and sell and make more money.' The agent said, 'Mr. Wolfe, you better listen to her.' I said, 'We will make some money on it—I can't make money staying at home working, but I can see that you make it.'

"Well, I can see that agent now—fine man. Mr. Wolfe said, 'Make the deed out to her and let her see what she can do with it.' He made the deed out to me. We did not sell the property, though. We turned it in and bought the next one to it on the corner. One day a man came along and put up a $100 option on that lot, and the man never came back, so Mr. Wolfe gained $100 on the lot. Later he sold the corner lot for $1,100."

I said, "You and Mr. Wolfe must have been pretty slick traders."

She looked at me shrewdly, her work-worn hands one upon the other in her lap. She said, "The half has never been told . . . We invested money in property on Ashland Avenue. We bought three lots down there and built three houses. One house we sold for $4,000 and the other two—I think we only got $3,000 for the other two. They were cheaper houses . . . You know, we had a boom in Asheville—before the Florida boom. We didn't enter into the boom. We loaned $20,000 out to others that went on the boom."

"Where did all that money come from?" I asked.

"From the sale of property and from what Mr. Wolfe made," she replied. "Others were in the boom and we loaned it to them. They lost it for us. Very little of it was ever paid back. They failed and didn't have any real estate security. We loaned T. S. Cobb $2,200 and John Bostick $300. We just had their notes. We got judgment against them. I nearly killed Bostick. He was willing to settle some way. He had some lots on Ore Street near the Southern Railroad Depot. It was no paved street. He had three lots down there, on Ore Street. They were on the corner. Two of them were on the corner and one above on another street. We built three houses on those lots. Two of them were sold. We sold one to a railroad man, a brakeman, who became an engineer afterwards. The man paid $250 down and so much every month. He paid it and we got a good profit and interest.

"We had a vacant lot down on Ore Street," she went on, "and railroad people built to that street. They came to me and said we want to buy that lot and I tell you what we will do—we will pay you $1,000 cash for it. 'All right,' Mr. Wolfe said, 'we want to get rid of it. They need it worse than we need the lot.' So I told the man, I told him, 'I have agreed to sell you the lot—you have the papers fixed up.' They paid $1,000 down for that lot. So on Ore Street we got rid of all that property down there."

For a few moments she was silent. It was a hot day and the shimmery heat waves danced above the rich Pennsylvania soil as we drove through the country.

"Yes, we made money and we lost it," she said, meditatively, with no overtone of regret that I could detect. "Way back there—that was about 1890—we had a big lot on Merman Avenue. It was 200 feet front and went back maybe 300 feet—very nice location. We held that lot and it took some little time. We had this lot and I wanted to build—we could build a good house for $10,000. Well, having lost money, that balked plans and I studied about all that money that should have gone into the house. I was going to save it again. I said he had some money and I had $3,000 in the First National Bank—yes, I said, we will build a house; we can start and finish it on the outside and leave the upstairs unfinished. Well, we studied it out and we got enough money to go ahead—and along came the crash and away went the bank—the bank failed in 1896.

"Fred was two years old and a few days, in August

—because Mother died in August. I can't say how much Mr. Wolfe had in that bank. He went nearly crazy, all that money gone again. I said, 'Only work with me now.' And oh, he raved, he said, 'You don't worry, we saved that money and someone else got it.'

"Well, I was not worried that we would go hungry. Of course we had property and we sold it. Mr. Wolfe was pretty broken up over everything, and nervous. He went to drinking. He claimed that I didn't worry enough. He got sick, he worried over things so. It took a lot of money to get him well . . ."

I stopped at a station for gas, and Mrs. Wolfe, catching sight of a garden of flowers adjacent to the driveway, got out and went over to inspect the blooms. She stood with that contemplative look of hers, her hands clasped in front of her. I took this moment of pause to tell her that the English department head at Lehigh University was having open house this afternoon for members of his staff, their wives and a number of students. I told her that I'd told him she was in Bethlehem and that he wanted very much to have her come, too. I told her they were using 'Look Homeward, Angel' as a text in the contemporary literature course at Lehigh.

She studied me closely. "What did you say his name was?—this man giving the party?"

I told her. She studied the flowers.

"Would you like to go?" I asked, in a moment.

"Why, yes, I'll go," she said.

I drove back to Bethlehem, to the Lehigh campus. On Professor Robert Smith's deep porch, shaded from the hot afternoon sun and overlooking the so-called "Christmas City," she sat surrounded by members of the English department, their wives, half a dozen students majoring in English.

They gazed at her. They were thinking: Eliza Gant in the flesh. And she sat there with the greatest self-possession in the world waiting for somebody to ask her to tell them about the great genius, fruit of her womb. For everywhere they asked her to tell them about Tom. She was accustomed to it.

A faculty wife—the gracious hostess type, a little too heavy on the gush—came up to her. "Mrs. Wolfe," she said, "if you only knew what this moment means to me. Your wonderful, wonderful son, Mrs. Wolfe! How fortunate we are to have you here!" And pausing to draw breath, she continued, "When October comes—always when October comes, I read the wonderful, beautiful lines your son wrote about October!"

"What is your name?" asked Mrs. Wolfe.

Taken aback, swallowing, the lady told her. She had been introduced to Mrs. Wolfe a few minutes before.

"How do you spell it?" asked Mrs. Wolfe.

The name was spelled, in a voice growing faint.

"I won't forget now," said Mrs. Wolfe. "You know, I never forget a name. That's why I make it a habit to get a name good and fixed in my mind."

But what about October? The faculty wife stood

there with her colored cheeks, smiling a little foolishly, and in a moment retreated to her seat. Everyone appeared as if seized with something like stage fright, excepting Mrs. Wolfe, who sat regarding her audience complacently.

Somebody said, "When Thomas was a child, did you have any idea that you had a genius on your hands?"

"Well, no, I didn't," replied Mrs. Wolfe. "Tom was a bright boy, but he would cling to you like a child, and I guess, as he said, I made a baby out of him because he was the last one of the family and the others were all older and could take care of themselves. If he wanted to go anywhere, he went with me. Mrs. Roberts knew he was a genius. She was teaching other boys, and she knew Tom—if Tom didn't show up as much as they wanted him to in school, it was because he was reading books. In 'Look Homeward, Angel' there was something about ancient philosophers, an argument, and Roberts said, 'Where did you get that?' Tom had told it, you know. It was that some one of them had never been married. This boy was the one that was helping Tom out in the argument—the Hildebrand boy it was."

Mrs. Wolfe paused; her lips moved without parting, as if she were trying to repress a smile. She said,

"Tom would go up to the library and get books as soon as he ate his lunch. He would be curled up on a lounge somewhere around the house reading. He never brought any of his school books home. I asked him about it, and he said, 'Oh, I've already prepared my lessons at the school.' The librarian said Tom took out more books than any boy in North Carolina. He didn't get children's books, either . . .

"Say, I'll tell you a story about Tom. It was when he was a little fellow, and I had a poisoned ankle from striking a coal bucket, and Dr. Glenn gave me a big dose of calomel. Oh, I had a poisoned limb, you know. Dr. Purefoy was the first doctor, and he kept me in agony for two months and a half, and one day he joked and said, 'Tom, we'll just have to strap her in and keep her off this leg.' Tom took the strap to hold the mattress on the bed, and said, 'Here doctor, here's a strap.' Thought the doctor meant it, you know, and we laughed.

"One morning he got to talking about Bible history. One of the patriarchs or something. He said, 'What is his name?' Well, I mentioned somebody. He had the biggest laugh. 'Oh, Mamma, that was two hundred years before that man was born,' he said. I said, 'Where did you learn those things?' And he said, 'Out of those Bible stories.' He didn't read the Bible so much, but he read the stories. He went to the play, 'Quo Vadis.' Mr. Wolfe took him, and Tom told him what was coming next. Mr. Wolfe said, 'That boy certainly remembers all he reads. He could tell the whole thing before they came on the stage.'

"Miss Mangum had a beau at my house one night, and Tom was curled up on the lounge reading, and they got talking about the Civil War and he went on to tell about some general, and Tom couldn't stand it any longer, and he said, 'No, you're mistaken.' Miss Mangum kind of grinned and said, 'I'll take Tom's word for it. I bet he's right.' This fellow said, 'I guess I was mistaken.' Miss Mangum certainly was all praise for Tom when he was a boy. She had tuberculosis and was delicate; she was a nurse. She married a man and then died several years afterwards."

Mrs. Wolfe's observant eyes glinted humorously now. She did not appear sunk in memories, but on the contrary fully appreciative of the fine attentive audience she had. She said,

"You know, Tom was emotional. He would jump up and down when he was well pleased. I said to him one day, 'Bring your books, we are going on a trip,' and he jumped up and down, he was so glad to go. Mr. Wolfe says, 'Leave him here. You are always dragging him out of school. He'll never get an education.' But Tom knew he was going, and he told Mrs. Roberts about it, and she said, 'How about that algebra?' And he said, 'Oh, but just think what I'll see on that trip!'

"I'll tell you something . . . Before we went to St. Louis—he was about three and one-half years old then. It was before we went out there—he and Max Israel were playing, and I let them have the band off the sewing machine we didn't use, and they rigged up a chair and played street car. The street cars hadn't been here so much then. Max was a smart boy, too. First they would talk about being conductor and motorman. Little tiny things, you know. One day Max changed. He said, 'Tom, I'll tell you what I'm going to be when I grow up. I guess I'll be a plumber like my daddy.' And Tom said, oh, he would rather be a United States general.

"Where he got that idea, the children would come home and speak of their history lessons, and Mr. Wolfe knew they were teaching Southern history. He liked the Southern generals; he came down south in the Reconstruction Days, and he became bitter against the North because he loved the Southern people and saw just how their pride was crushed, and a lot of carpetbaggers were sent down. Perhaps it wasn't the fault of Washington. They tried to do so much; they sent the wrong people very often. But Mr. Wolfe admired the South all the way through—Jeb Stuart, Robert E. Lee, Fitzhugh Lee, and all those Southern generals, and he would speak about General so and so. That was where Tom got it, because he had heard Mr. Wolfe speak about it.

"And way back there Mr. Wolfe saw Fitzhugh Lee himself. They were marching into Gettysburg, just before the battle. They marched all day long in front of the house, and Mr. Wolfe was only a little boy, though they all had to work then. The horses were pretty well played out, and they would send them back to the farms to recuperate, and he would watch the horses, and they had them hid over there, afraid the Rebels would steal them.

"Well, along came these two men, not with the others, and ordered him, 'Say, take us to a good spring; we want some water.' He was scared to death, but he took them up to the spring, and handed one of them a big gourd of water. The man drank it and said, 'Come on, I'm going to take you to Jeb Stuart,' and the other man said, 'He is teasing you, he isn't going to take you. That's Fitzhugh Lee you gave the water to. He isn't going to take you.'

"I could tell you how bitter he was long after the war was over . . . This man was going to build the penitentiary in Raleigh and finish the State House at Columbia, South Carolina. Mr. Ware was coming down to take this contract, and he said, 'Billy,'—he called Mr. Wolfe Billy—his name was William Oliver—'don't you want to go South with me? Down to Raleigh and Columbia?' Well, Mr. Wolfe packed his things and went up home, and his mother screamed and cried, 'Oh, those awful Rebels will murder you if you go down there. I'll never see you alive again.' But that's what he wanted; he wanted the experience, and he came. They kept writing him to come away from those people down there. He went back north after a while and stayed at a place called Boiling Springs in Pennsylvania, and then he sold his things all out and said, 'I'll never stay in such a country as this.' So he came back to the South, and his mother screamed and cried again . . . I think I smoothed it all over. We went up there about a year and a half after we were married, and they just opened their arms to me. I was a different Southerner, and you know that old lady spoke bitterly of Mr. Wolfe's other wives. Mr. Wolfe was afraid she would insult them, because she was so bitter against the Rebels, that was why he hadn't taken either of them up there. But when I went, everything was fine. She wasn't bitter against the South any more. She said, 'George,' that was her grandson, 'came down South and stayed a year and they sent him home. Mrs. Allen and Cynthia didn't want him.' Well, I happened to know something about that."

Mrs. Wolfe looked from one to another mysteriously, and there was triumph too in her expression.

"Yes, I knew about that," she said. "The truth of the matter about George . . . Cynthia's sister-in-law had come to stay there, too, and her husband was in Morristown. She was a pretty woman—a fickle woman— and liked George's company, and they went visiting back and forth over the town together, and they just thought he was becoming infatuated or something. Her name was Ella Hill. You can't tell about people, you know. I met her husband, John, and they seemed very devoted to each other. Mr. Wolfe said it was 'honey' and 'sugar' and everything like that. They didn't have

any family or any children. She liked to live easy—
didn't want to do any work.

"Well, I told Mr. Wolfe about his mother saying
that Mrs. Allen and Cynthia were the ones sent George
home. I said, 'The truth of the matter is, you were the
one that sent him home, Mr. Wolfe. You were jealous.'
George was a younger man, and Mr. Wolfe didn't like
it. Mr. Wolfe's mother had the wrong impression about
the whole thing. She fairly worshipped George. His
father was killed in the war, and the mother died when
he was three months old, with a broken heart, and of
course the grandmother raised him. They all said she
thought more of the grandchild than she did of any of
her own children. She said George was a good boy, he
never gave her any impudence. But I heard about why
they sent him home. It was because he liked Ella that
they sent him home. George bragged on Ella, said she
was the only one that cared for him down there. Ella
had a pretty face . . . It was a funny way to live,
though," she added thoughtfully.

One of the students cleared his throat, and said,
"Who was Cynthia, Mrs. Wolfe?"

"Why, she was Mr. Wolfe's wife, his second wife,"
Mrs. Wolfe explained.

The student looked perplexed. "Then—were you his
third?"

Mrs. Wolfe's lips worked tremulously, but her eyes
were humorous. "Yes, I was Mr. Wolfe's third. No
doubt he had had lots of girl friends. He said one girl

did without anything to eat for a whole week because she thought he was going to marry her. Cynthia's first cousin. He had had so many love affairs."

She shook her head, her expression on the moment rather severe: "You scatter your love, and there isn't much love. You get immune. But he was a good family man, though. I could have gotten anything in the world out of Mr. Wolfe by just flattering him a little. But I was stubborn. I couldn't do it. I knew what I could do, but I didn't . . . It was like the time he first drank. He said forgive and forget and not to think of it any more. I said, 'If you never drink any more, in time I'll forget, and I might forgive.' But I couldn't forget things that maybe he had said and all that. Maybe I was to blame. It was just meanness maybe, but I couldn't do it."

In the pause which ensued, the student who had spoken before—a lad with ingenuous open gaze—now said, "Who was this Ella, Mrs. Wolfe, this girl you spoke of a minute ago?"

"Why, she was Cynthia's brother's wife," replied Mrs. Wolfe. "As I say, she was just fickle, lived on praise and whatever could flatter her. That was about all she had. The dull type. Mrs. Allen, her mother-in-law, told me about her. Her husband was a clerk at Morristown, Tennessee, at a hotel, and he came after her and took her. He was completely sold on me—I treated him well. He told Mrs. Allen, 'I'm going back and send Ella up there.' Well, Mrs. Allen said to me,

'It won't do for her to come, you write the letter for me, and we'll stop her.' She couldn't write, she was getting up in years. Well, Ella didn't come. I told her in the letter that he had had a nice visit and enjoyed himself, and I was glad he had. So she wrote me a letter, sharp and sarcastic, and said she wanted to tell me I was welcome to all I got. Of course, Mr. Wolfe didn't know I wrote the letter. When her letter came, he was furious about it because she had said that."

Refreshments were served, and Mrs. Wolfe sipped of her non-alcoholic drink.

"Mrs. Wolfe," somebody said, "tell us some more about your son. How did he happen to go into writing?"

"Well, he always had a liking for reading and writing," Mrs. Wolfe replied. "We planned that he would go to college, and after he finished school Mrs. Roberts, or somebody, put it in his head that he ought to take a higher course. And then somebody had put it in his head that the University of Virginia had a higher rating than Chapel Hill—and Mr. Wolfe says, 'You aren't going to Virginia. You are a North Carolinian and you are going to patronize your own State. I'm going to pay for it, and you are going where I want you to go.'

"Tom was back in the dining room one day and he said, 'They tell me that Virginia has a higher rating,' and I said, 'Tom, let me tell you something. Your papa's going to pay for it, and you go on down to Chapel Hill this year, and then if you want to switch over next year it will be all right, but he is determined. You go down there where he wants you to go, or you'll go to work. Chapel Hill's all right. You will like it.'

"Well, Tom never thought about changing after he went down. But that is how it happened. I said, 'You go on down, and if you want to go to Virginia, it will be easy to switch over there. I know your papa.' I knew Mr. Wolfe could pay for it and save me from paying it. But I paid for Harvard. Mr. Wolfe said, 'No. You have been through the University; that is more than most boys in town get. I am through. I can't afford any more.' Tom said to me, 'I'm going to Harvard if I have to borrow the money.' And I said, 'You go on up there—I'll pay for it.' He went to Harvard three years . . . I had had experience with Mr. Wolfe.

"And that's the way it was. Mr. Wolfe wanted him to be a lawyer. Tom thought he would try it out. He went up to Haywood Parker, a prominent lawyer, getting along up in years now, and he told him, 'I want to follow journalism, but Papa wants me to be a lawyer.' And Mr. Parker said, 'By all means, if you have a talent or feeling for journalism, take that up. There's lots of room at the top, but there are too many lawyers right now. So many of them don't amount to anything. There's plenty of room for you, so I would take journalism if I had a talent in that direction.'

"I've been thinking of going up to his office and talking to him. I think he is chairman of that cemetery company, and there are lots out there that have curbing around them, and I want to see if he can't put this curbing on the walkway in front of the Westall lot and ours, too. We had to take a tree down right where Tom's marker is. We had to go see Haywood Parker about that, and he gave Atwood—that's the sexton— gave him orders to take it down. I think by going to see him I can get the curbing. I'm going to tell him what Tom said—that he gave Tom the idea of going into journalism, and that was the cause of his going into writing . . .

"Well, the summer after Tom graduated from Chapel Hill they needed an English teacher at Bingham Military School, and they wrote Chapel Hill and Tom was recommended. Mr. Wolfe was sick, and Tom wanted to go to Harvard and not teach. But of course he said he would stay that year since his papa was likely to die. He hated to be way off in Boston. Well, they sent the car in and took Tom out to see the old Colonel Bingham, and they told me Tom said, 'I'll go back and talk to Mother and let you know what she says.' And the Colonel said, 'That boy will make his way in the world. He wants to see what his mother says about it, and he's going to side with her.' In a few days they sent for Tom again, and Tom told them he wanted to go into journalism, and he was afraid to commence teaching, and wanted to go to Harvard, but on account of his father's sickness he would not go.

"And you know, they said if he would teach there a year, they'd see that he got into journalism. Of course that sounded pretty well. You know Bingham is an educated man, a writer and a speaker, and all. Well, we talked it over, and the doctor was here one night and Tom said, 'Doctor, do you think Papa might die this year?' 'Oh,' the doctor says, 'why do you ask that?—we can't tell you.' And Tom says, 'I can stay here and teach this year if he is likely to pass on, but I want to go to Harvard.' And the doctor said, 'Why boy, go on to Harvard. Why your Papa might outlive you and me both. To look at him, his chances aren't as good as ours. He is a sick man, but don't stand back on that account. You go, if you want to go to Harvard.'

"And that's what decided Tom. He went right on that fall. He graduated in two years, but he took the next year with Professor Baker, and he would have gotten home in time to see Mr. Wolfe, but he was over in Boston when we sent him the wire to come at once, and when he got back that night late, he found the telegram, but he had no money, and there was no train, and he had to wait until the next morning to get his money."

The long warm afternoon wore away as Mrs. Wolfe talked. No provision had been made for serving an evening meal to the some twenty-odd persons present, and with the approach of supper-time they began to go. Mrs. Wolfe nibbled at what remained of a cracker she had been given earlier, and sipped at the purple fluid in her glass.

"Are we ready to go?" I whispered.

She rose. Professor Smith brought out a copy of "Of

Time and the River" for her to autograph. He placed
it upon a stand and held the pen ready. In her deliber-
ate, unhurried way she took the pen and made ready
to write. She looked at the book contemplatively. Presently she began to write.

In the automobile I asked her if she could eat a
steak.

"Well, I reckon I could," she said.

The news got around that Thomas Wolfe's mother was in Bethlehem. That same evening three school teachers and a librarian called me and asked if they could come to see her. I asked Mrs. Wolfe if she was willing, and she said sure let them come, the more the merrier.

"When?"

"Why, tonight, of course," she said.

"But after being at Lehigh all afternoon, aren't you tired?"

"Tired? I don't know what it means," she said. "The day before I left home there was this woman came to see me, and I talked until twenty minutes of three in the morning. I didn't get tired. I got sleepy. You know what was the matter?—I had eaten four or five times during the day, but I don't eat much at the time. The last I had eaten was maybe five or six o'clock, and when I went back to my room I had a headache, and I happened to think, 'Yes, it's food I need.' And it was three o'clock before I went to bed, and I made coffee and ate something or other and drank some milk, and my head didn't ache anymore . . .

"I tell you—they'd better come tonight," she added, "because I am going tomorrow."

"Going?" I asked, taken aback. "Going back home?"

"Well, I'll stop at Washington and see Mabel, and then I'll go on home," she said. "I've got a million things to do—the garden and the house and all, so I'll just be on my way, as the fellow says, in the morning."

So the teachers and the librarian came that evening and sat in the parlor and looked at the mother of a man who wrote famous novels. She got started talking about her St. Louis venture of 1904:

"When you have children and when you sew and work for a family you have enough to do to keep busy," she said. "Mr. Wolfe went to so many sanitariums about that time. Tom was born in 1900. Well, I still worked and Mr. Wolfe got so awfully nervous. The girls had grown up and gone to school and could be of help to me—the children were a lot of help and Effie and Mabel pitched in and helped, too. I was saving money by not hiring anybody else to do it.

"Mr. Wolfe was nervous—he sat and drank. He said, 'Why don't you do something?' Well, of course I hadn't kept up with teaching, I couldn't get a school or anything. And I couldn't leave the family. I kept boarders. I really do not know what I could do more than I was doing, and I told him that. I talked to him in his sober moments. 'If you stop your drinking and carry on business you will be all right,' I told him. I said, 'When the children are grown, why then we can do something.'

"I had been reading about the World's Fair and the children wanted to go to St. Louis—young Wesley was out there and talked about it to Ollie and his wife. They were there in 1904, in the spring, in April. I said, 'I believe I will go out and rent a house. I will get a house. The children will see the Fair and they will be away from you,' I said to Mr. Wolfe.

"Well, I left Effie and Frank, the older ones, and took five—Mabel, Grover, Fred, Ben and Tom—Tom was three and a half years old, and we rented a house. I paid $200 a month for the house. I did not fall down on the rent. They required the rent in advance, I had to pay each month in advance. Well, and I did that.

"A number of people came and stayed. I sent back $500 to Mr. Wolfe. I said that to offset the first money I brought out here I have sent that back to him and am going to have another $500 for him. The children went to the Fair. Grover and Fred were the business men. Ben and Grover, the twins, did not make a team working together. Ben was reserved. Grover and Fred, though, they worked together. They went to Inside Inn, and along the paths and fruit stands they cleared down a place where you go into the inside into the dining room. It was the kind of hotel that was built just for the World's Fair.

"And those boys sold newspapers for the Union News Company right next to the fruit stand, and everybody passed going into the dining room. The children told me, 'They just take our papers off the counter.' People naturally want newspapers. Fred would laugh about it. The customers did not take the change. The papers cost two cents and sold for five. Some laid out twenty-five cents cash right along. The children would go back and count up the money and pay the man two cents for a paper. The other money was theirs, and they brought as much as $4 each home in a day's time.

"Well, I considered that they made money, and I kept the money for them. Miss Moore and her father came to St. Louis. Mr. Moore was an honest man, I gave him $150 of Grover's, Ben's and Fred's to take back and put in the bank. I said, 'Give me your vest,' and I put that money inside and sewed the vest flat so nobody would know, even if they had held him up. He gave Mr. Wolfe this $150 and he put it in the bank to the boys' credit. Then Mr. Jones, a reliable man—he worked for the Asheville Woodworking Company—he came, and he and his family were there. I sent $250 back with him. He said, 'All right, I will deliver it to Mr. Wolfe.' He gave me a receipt and he took the money back to Mr. Wolfe."

She was silent and watched the Boston terrier move across the floor for a cooler spot to lie down in greater comfort (if that was possible, the night so warm).

"Then Grover got sick," she went on, "and Mr. Wolfe came out, and I think I had $900. Of course we had some expenses to pay. But I did not care for money any more after Grover died. We came home. We left things I had bought for the house, just left it. The man who owned the house got it.

"We got back home November nineteenth. He died on the sixteenth. We were expecting to go home the end of November, because they had extended the Fair another month, and I had paid up until the end of November. But we went home then.

"I could have given up any child I had and it could not have hurt any worse. I could not take an interest in anything. Mr. Wolfe thought I should paint and paper the house—we had $3,000. I said, 'I cannot even talk about papering. Do it any way you want to do it.'

"He painted the house. After that I tried to get interested in Tom. It was a sad time for Tom. It might have affected him for the worse, too. Well, we had this Owenby place, and the North Presbyterian Mission Board had come to buy it. They were people from the North, and they wanted this house for a mission school. We sold them thirteen acres at a pretty good price—the Owenby place.

"Well, this minister came to see me about the house and talk over the property. He said, 'Your sorrow is great, but you have the other children. Now I will tell you—I lost my wife,' he said, 'and I lost my mother and one child, all in three months' time. I do not know why God has required it of me. I live only to work, to do church work. That is the only way you can do— keep busy and work. You cannot brood.' He said, 'You must forget, and work.' He was right. Commencing with the end of 1904 and the beginning of 1905 to the end of the next summer I went around and looked at different places. Mr. Campbell, the agent, took me over to Chestnut Street and showed me one place, and I wasn't satisfied. The house did not appeal to me—was old and too far away from the Woodfin Street house. I said, 'I will hold the family together and keep one place.'

"Well, the next afternoon the agent came down to the house, and he said, 'Mrs. Wolfe, I think I have just what you want. The Meyers place.' T. M. Meyers. A man from Kentucky. He was a lecturer, a Campbellite preacher, and a very brainy man at one time, but he snapped several times they said, and had to go to an institution. I said to Mr. Wolfe, 'This Meyers place is for sale,' and Mrs. Meyers showed me through. Mr. Wolfe said, 'Do you want it?' I said, 'Yes, but I don't want to say we will take it without you.' Mr. Wolfe said, 'Jack, she wants it, make the papers out to her. If she is satisfied, I don't care.'

"Well, the next day the papers were ready. I went to the office of Bernard and Bernard, two lawyers. It took

one-half hour for the sale. I took over nineteen boarders. They were in the house when I bought it."

She looked at the teachers and the librarian, one after the other. She fixed her gaze upon me.

"I was busy trying to pay off after that. I wanted to
pay it off. We still had the Owenby place over country.
We had vegetables from that place. We had the Woodfin Street place and had a garden out there. I kept the
table all next summer mostly from our own garden. I
boarded the family. The children came over, and Mr.
Wolfe came by for breakfast. Tom stayed with me. I
had a poisoned limb, the poison was just above the shoe
top, just below the calf of the leg, over the shoe top. It
was about the size of a pea, of ink red color and a
white ring inside directly in the center. For a week or
two there was pain and swelling in my leg. I sent for
the doctor and he made me go to bed.

"I had a cot put in the kitchen. I could sit up on the
cot and do things, and the boarding house carried on. I
could sit up on the cot and do a lot of things. I could
string the beans to cook for dinner. I said, 'Bring me
everything in the laundry to be mended.' And along
came my sister-in-law to see me. She said she had a rolling chair. She said, 'Send the colored boy over for it
and you can have it—you can get in the rolling chair
and roll down the hall.' So I sent over for the chair. I
could roll around in it, my leg hanging down. Dr. Purefoy kept coming in and left directions for me to follow.

I didn't stay in bed, though. I went to the kitchen and rolled back and forth. And you know, the leg commenced to swell and got inflamed. It turned blue. It was just terrific.

"Mr. Wolfe saw my condition and called the doctor. He said, 'Doctor, it looks like her leg has to come off.' The doctor came and he told me he had orders to take the leg off. I said, 'The leg stays with me. My leg goes when I go.' "

She smiled. "But as the saying goes, I survived . . . All the pain—I said, 'Dr. Purefoy, what could have caused it?' She nodded grimly and looked triumphant. She said, "I was in that chair about two and a half months—but I survived it . . .

"All the way back there—and the things that have happened since. Money made and money gone. There's Florida now . . . I went down there in January, 1923. I had pneumonia in December, after Mr. Wolfe died . . .

"Miami Beach had a fine view. I was so impressed with Miami Beach I could not understand why everybody did not go down and buy a winter home. I was among the first people in the country to think of that. Fisher's head man said I had more foresight than anyone he knew. Miami Beach had about 1600 inhabitants. The Breakers was the only hotel. I had foresight about what Miami Beach was going to be, and I bought property after property.

"I picked up a property and paid $10,000 for it. I sold that in forty-five days for $16,000. It was gambling, and I had turned it in too soon. Everything I touched, someone else wanted it in less than no time. I bought so much of it and I could sell it, and during the summer of 1925 there was a great boom time, but I was in Asheville and did not know it. And not knowing Miami was on boom, I got on the train—the day William Jennings Bryan was found dead in bed at Dayton, Tennessee, at Stokes Hall—that day I was on the train to see Mr. Thomas of the Miami Trust Company—I wanted to see Mr. Thomas about some papers locked in his private safe.

"Two ladies from St. Louis and I had gone across the aisle to look over the scenery, and three young men came in and looked around for a seat. It was a Pullman train—I did not travel any other way then. I said I would not move—they were only real estate men. A fellow—he was from Minnesota—he sat down and started to talk, and he said, 'Are you ladies going down to buy property in Miami?' I said, 'Neither buying nor selling—we're going down on business.' He said, 'Have you reservations?—they are very much crowded.' I said, 'I am going on business and do not need reservations.'

"Well, they went away, and after a while this young man came back and said, 'Your remark about neither buying nor selling leads me to believe you own property. Where?' I told him the best property on the beach. I was independent. I did not tell him much. He hemmed and hawed. Finally he said, 'I have a friend interested in beach property and he is buying property down there. You may be able to sell it to him.'

"I said, 'Summer is not the best time to sell—winter is the best time. I will hold it until winter.' He said, 'Sell any time you can get a good price.' He said, 'I will meet you in the morning.' I said, 'I have to go to the bank in the morning.' He said, 'I will take you to the bank.' I said, 'I know the way down there, and it will be a pleasure to walk—it is only three blocks anyhow.' "

Mrs. Wolfe paused, fingered her nose thoughtfully.

"The next morning," she continued, "I got out of the Pullman and was going to the Miami Hotel for breakfast, and a man said, 'Hello.' He said, 'I met you on the train,' and I saw it was the same one and felt he was annoying to me. I tried every way to get rid of him. He said he had a car and would take me to the bank. I said, 'I want to stop at a friend's real estate office on Second Street.'

"When I got out of the car, he left the car and came to see what real estate office I went in to. He stayed so long his car was taken by the police. So he said. He asked me to wait for him—he said he had to get the car. I said, 'No, I'm going to the bank to see about some papers.' Well, this man watched for me over at the

Plaza Hotel. It was a hot July day. He said, 'Get in my car and go with me and get cooled off.' Well, I sat up front with him and we went over to the Beach. He said he wanted to see property on the beach. I told him about my lots, but did not say anything about what price I wanted. He said, 'I do not think they are worth $10,000 apiece, but they are worth $9,000.' I did not know there was a boom on—he was just there offering to buy.

"I showed him another lot. We were over on the ocean front. These lots were on the bay of Indian Creek where the yacht races are run—you cannot tie up a yacht on the ocean side. The lot was a hundred feet front by two hundred and thirty-six feet deep—a good big lot. I did not get out of the car, I was so independent.

"He parked and got out and walked around. I said I was already offered $27,000 for it, and would not take a penny less than $30,000 for it. He climbed in and said, 'I will give you $30,000. What are your terms?' And I said, 'Cash, $10,000 and the other in two years.' And I said, 'I do not like to part with any of my lots—you said you'd give $30,000 for it, but I have not said I'd sell it to you.'

"We crossed the bridge and went over on Pine Tree Drive. I said, 'Well, I made a good deal of money on three other lots on Pine Tree Drive.' I said, 'There is one lot left, a corner lot, but I am planning to build a

home on it—it is not for sale.' And he said, 'What else
have you?' I said, 'I am not going to say anything else.
I will go back to Miami.'

"I stopped back at Fisher's office and Hugh Larry
came up to me. He said, 'I have been offered $35,000
for your lot.' And I looked at him, and said, 'Well, I
told that man over there that I'd sell for $30,000.' He
said, 'Go to a lawyer—they have held you up.' 'Well,'
I said, 'take me back to Miami Hotel.'

"I went upstairs and was getting freshened up. I
heard a typewriter just going downstairs. They were
drawing up the contract for the property . . ."

Mrs. Wolfe's eyes glittered with the opiate of property gambling. She went on and on, telling of her trad-
ings, her gains and loses, until it made one's head spin.
In her enthusiasm she played hob with chronology, going back and forth on the calendar like a cat on the
keys:

"The eighth of January, 1923, I went to Miami for
the first time. Fisher was just putting on some develop-
ments. He was going to develop Miami and all around.
There was a young man—John Frazer. Two years before John had come to Asheville and stopped at my
house, and I had kept in touch with him. He came up
and stayed. He said, 'Mrs. Wolfe, I bought three lots
in Miami and I need some more money, and I will sell
you the property for just what I paid for it.' I said,
'John, has it any security?' John said he had no secu-

rity. Well, John and Fred had been coming up for several years, and John had paid $8,000 in on it, so I paid his equity out. I said I am not sending fourteen dollars a month down there every month. I wrote George Meredity to fix up the abstract, and I'd pay the whole thing off. About that time Jesse Law was taking a tour. I said, 'Mr. Law, I bought property and I wish you could go attend to this. I will send you a check.' I gave Jesse Law the money to get the abstract—it was moral law—and I paid it off in two years.

"After Mr. Wolfe died in June, Dr. Glenn said go to Florida or you will be in the cemetery before the end of spring. I went. Mabel and Ralph had gone down and Ralph was coming back to stay with his mother. Mabel told John Frazer I was coming down. She always said, 'Mamma's real estate friend.' John was there at Green Tree Inn. He said he wanted to take me out to Cocoanut Grove, it was a nice old place. There was a new development put on—not more than ninety-six lots in the whole development. He took me out there to this development. There was one place—it was never anywhere but the most beautiful section that he showed me—there was a grove of fruit trees. Well, of course I just decided on a corner lot. I said, 'I will take the corner lot for myself and the next one for Fred.' I think my lot was about $1,500 and Fred's $800. I said, 'I will take these two lots and have grapefruit and avacado pears right on my lot.' I never tasted anything like those grapefruit. Delicious! Well, I was to have all the fruit

I could eat. They wanted to buy the trees. They said, 'We will take $100 off the lot if you leave the fruit on the trees.'

"That was the first day's venture. It was signed up before I went to bed that night. The next morning people came to see me. Mabel said, 'Mamma, four men are waiting to take you out to see real estate.' I said, 'I can't go with all at one time.' But I said, 'Don't worry, I will go with all of you and see what you have—but I don't promise to buy.'

"In two weeks I was perfectly well—all over my sickness. John took me over to the beach and he sold that lot over just past the place where the Plaza is now, but there wasn't any house there, except the houses that belonged to Pancoast's father. I bought the lot. I looked all around, and he said that site is for a hotel. I said, 'You real estate gentlemen say anything to make a deal.' But I took the lot. I did not sleep well that night. Dr. Perry had fallen down on his payments and wanted to sell. I paid this other man, but both had to be in the deal when they sold. I said, 'If they cannot see anything in it, why did I buy it?' I thought, 'The place will be a hotel some day—I will build me a home on it, and if hotels come, I will get a fortune.' Three other agents had filed in at Green Tree. Mr. Patey wanted to take me out and show me property. He took me out to Fifty-Fourth Street. They were building two or three little houses—$6,000 each. He said, 'Let me sell you the block.' There were thirty-six lots in the block. I

said, 'Away out in pines and away from civilization?'
He said, 'It is cheap enough.' I said, 'If it is not well
located, nothing is cheap. It is away from civilization
—west of Iowa—take me where white folks go. This
does not interest me at all.'

"So he says, 'The beach property is the best.' He said,
'We have some property over there—come on.' He took
me. It was up from the water front and over the bay
right about midway between Indian Creek and Biscay
Bay. He said, 'I will sell you a lot right in the center
for $13,000.' I figured I could double it—make $25,000
next winter. Well, next morning I called up Fisher's
office. We had moved from the hotel because of the
noise. I got a room at Mrs. Jacoby's—$15 a week, on
the third floor. Mrs. Jacoby had no phone. I went to the
Levington Hotel and paid ten cents for a call to Miami
Beach and called Fisher's office. Mr. Worth answered
me, said, 'I will come over in a little while and show
you what we have.'

"Mr. Worth took me down between two islands. I
said, 'I will look between the two islands and then look
against them. What are your terms?' He said $7,500
apiece—$15,000 for the two. He went on to figure. He
said $3,000 down. The next day this agent went to the
main office and got the man that runs the office. They
figured it up. At dinner the agent said, 'Mr. Patey tells
me he sold you some property over here.' Well, I found
out he was at the head of the whole thing.

"Well, I went home and gave them a check for

$1,000. They gave me the papers. I wanted a deed, and would let him have a mortgage for $3,700 when everything was finished. He said it would be three months—they would take the deed down and record it.

"About two weeks from that time I had a wire from Mr. Law, saying, 'I am coming to Tennessee to see a party.' I wired, 'Come out here, be glad to see you.' Well, when he came, he had this agent for old Patey with him. I said, 'Well, where do *you* come from?' I was sitting in the car talking to Law. And he said, 'If you had been in Miami last Friday you would have made a fortune—you should have heard us sell property.' The party with old Patey said, 'Why, we sold out Fair Green. Geiger wanted a place on the beach—they are going to build a big place there,' and he spread out a map and showed me.

"I said, 'This is over on the beach where I bought two lots. Why,' I said, 'I have a deed to that property!'

"He said, 'Your deed is not on record.' I said, 'I paid him for recording the deed and paid him the first $1,000, and a check afterward.' I said, 'This is not according to law.' He said, 'I think I can give you $4,000.' I said, 'Why, I'd sell it and double the money. They have to pay me if they want that old Pelican Hotel built there.' He said he wired his office and the agent at the office had said he would give me three other lots for this if I wanted it, but would only hold it until next Wednesday, three days off.

"Mabel said, 'Mamma, what is your direction?' I said, 'Well, wire this man that I am on the next train.' And I left the next day and went down. The next thing I went to see a lawyer. I went to the First National Bank of Miami and got a lawyer—his name was Pierce. I told him the situation. He said, 'We will have to bring suit.' I said, 'If they'd give me $5,000, I'd call it off.' Geiger, the man who owned the property, could not do it. The agent had not told him. The agent had made a telephone report. Well, the only thing was to bring suit. I said, 'I will bring suit for $10,000'—the court granted two years' time. In the meantime, I had bought this lot from John Frazer.

"I sent a check to the lawyer. Then I said, 'Well, is there any way we can make a deal with Geiger. I do not like law suits.' He said, 'Of course I know Gus Geiger.' He called him. He said, 'Gus, Mrs. Wolfe is at my office. We want to talk this matter all over again.' He said, 'We want to settle this some other way, out of court.' And Geiger said, 'I will give her three lots for the two she first bought for $1,300.' And the lawyer said, 'We know you are in for it because you endorsed that $1,000 check—you endorsed it, so you knew you had sold it.' Geiger said Pancoast came over to the real estate office and said where is Mrs. Wolfe. Parker said she has gone home. He said, 'Wire her to come back, we have to buy those lots from her—we will sell the hotel property—we will sell everything on the strength of this hotel being there.' He said, 'She is just an old lady—just give her three lots over there—she won't care. We must have that hotel here.'

"Well, Geiger said he would give me the three lots for $9,000. Geiger was willing to do anything to get it settled. I said, 'I have not done anything wrong—but somebody has made a crooked deal, and it has been a great shock to me.' I said, 'The hotel will never be built on that lot—you will never have a hotel there—as you mete it shall be measured unto you.' The plans were drawn up—there were seventy-odd developments. I said, 'Understand, your hotel will never be built there —you will never have a Pelican Hotel there.'

"I paid one payment on the lots. The hotel did not seem to be progressing. He said, 'Mrs. Wolfe, I will tell you—I have lost $10,000 on it.' He said, 'Of course there is to be no hotel built there—with income tax and everything it is too much.'

"I went back home in two weeks. I got my principal back. I had bought two more from Fisher before I left —on the ocean front. When I went back next fall, Mrs. Howe from Ohio wanted ocean front lots. I said sell her the lots—I said I will not lose any money. It all put a bad taste in my mouth and I said, 'I will let her have them, I will get rid of them. I paid $11,300 for them and sold them for $20,000. She paid $20,000, and taxes and interest. When I went down there, Fisher's Number One agent gave me a look and said, 'I am

so glad to see you—I haven't seen you in four years.'
They said I started the boom. They put it in the newspaper—in headlines . . ."

Mrs. Wolfe ceased speaking. She looked around, re-
alizing suddenly that she had lost her audience. The
teachers and the librarian were talking in undertones
together, apparently discussing affairs of their own,
nothing to do with Mrs. Wolfe. For a spell Mrs. Wolfe
sat there, the stream of life passing her by.

She looked at me. She gave me a beckoning finger.
I drew my chair close and she shielded her words behind her hand:

"You asked me," she said, "what Tom meant that
time—in the book—about not being the last . . ."

Her small brown eyes had a bright, mysterious look.

"Yes," I said.

"Well, I'll tell you," she said in her husky whisper.

I bent closer.

"But it's strictly off the record," she said.

"Yes," I breathed.

"Off the record," she said.

I promised.

She told me, whispering behind her hand. It was a
terrible and extraordinary thing—an account of mis-
carriage under circumstances bordering on horror. She
etched the narrative in spare, powerful strokes, con-
juring up swiftly a stark, unforgetable episode, a

purple flower of tragic conflict and heroic fortitude. And meanwhile the teachers and the librarian sat there in polite and subdued tête-à-tête, discussing something earnestly, never suspecting.

The next morning she stood on the landing platform in front of the American Hotel, at Broad and New Streets, waiting for a Philadelphia bus. She would change at Philadelphia for Washington, she said, stop over to see Mabel in Washington, and then on home.

I can see her now, a determined and unhurried elderly lady in black, a white scarf around her neck, standing solidly planted on the platform. Like a rock, and the waves of new generations passing on the streets.

On the bus she found a seat. She looked back at me, smiling with lips that made little movements in spite of being pressed firmly together. She winked with one eye, roguishly, as the vehicle bore her away.